Affliction

dpInk: DonnaInk Publications, L.L.C.

dpInk
DonnaInk Publications, L.L.C.

United States of America

Affliction

by

DOTTIE DANIELS

Published in 2015 by dpInk: Donnalnk Publications, L.L.C.
129 Daisy Hill Road, Carthage, North Carolina 28327
Copytright © 2015 by dpInk: Donnalnk Publications, L.L.C. for Ms. Dottie Daniels.
Printed in the United States of America
International Standard Book Number: 978-1-939425-54-6 (ack. pbk.)
International Standard Book Number: 978-1-939425-58-4 (ack. digital)

"Twenty-six year old, bi-racial paramedic SEANNA BURGES wakes up five hours late to the sound of breaking glass on what was to be the eighth and final day of her work stretch. Seanna has been informed by Ronny that the hospital they both work at has been overrun with infected patients since the early morning hours and checking in to work is both useless and dangerous. She is subsequently bitten and her infection reacts differently than the other victims - for one important reason - she remains alive." by Author.

1st Edition. This is a work of fiction. Names, characters, places, brands, media, and incidents are either the product of the author's imagination or are used fictitiously. Any resemblance to actual persons either living or dead, events, or locales are purely coincidental.

Library of Congress Cataloging-in-Publication Data

Catalog record is depicted here and also available from the Library of Congress

12 11 10 9 8 7 6 5 4 3 2 1

Daniels, Dottie.

Affliction / Dottie Daniels

176 p. cm.

2013936125

1) Literature - Fiction, 2) Horror – Fiction 3) Apopcalyptic – Fiction, 4) Monster - Fiction, 5) Science Fiction - Fiction, 6) Futurist - Fiction, 7) Zombie - Fiction, 8) Medical Disaster - Fiction, 9) United States - Fiction, 10) Minnesota - Fiction.

Visit dpInk: Donnalnk Publications, L.L.C. at:
www.donnaink.com
(888) 564-7741 (office) | (800) 861-6512 (fax)
129 Daisy Hill Road, Carthage, North Carolina 28327

CONTENTS

DEDICATION

For Gramps.

Affliction

Chapter One

I woke up five hours later than my usual five-thirty alarm initiated rising. It was Thursday, the last day of my eight day work stretch, which was supposed to begin at seven a.m. and end twelve hours later. I'd been working these twelve-hour shifts for the last four days in a row with the intention of making a nice contribution toward our vacation this summer once my boyfriend Graham went on break from his graduate studies. My eight-day stretch started out strong with the regular eight-hour shifts but yesterday after three days of overtime, I felt a tingle in my throat. Convinced it was the beginnings of a cold from our rainier than usual May precipitation, I took to the medicine cabinet last night before Graham left my apartment in Allentown, PA for his rental house in the neighboring town of Bethlehem, just before eleven. I had taken what I thought was a magic combination of cold and flu tablets and some cough syrup for my sore throat. The last thing I remember was cuddling up with Graham, listening to his upcoming plans for a possible camping trip while watching Jimmy Kimmel Live. Needless to say, after taking the cold medicine I didn't hear him leave my bedroom, much less my apartment that night. We had exchanged house keys over a year ago so it was not unusual at all.

I was jolted awake by a loud scream coming from a woman, followed by her sobbing, and then silence. Right after that I heard glass shatter outside from what must've been a car window being smashed because the car alarm sounded immediately afterwards. As I was scrambling to get the sheets and the comforter from being wrapped around me so I could go look out of my bedroom window, I heard again more noise, this time coming from inside in the form of a man yelling within the apartment building. I couldn't hear what he said at first but it ended with, "Man I know you hear me! What the hell is wrong with you? Get away from me, man!" followed by a slamming door. That was more of a distraction than the outside commotion because even though the rent was reasonable, the apartment building was pretty quiet and this kind and amount of noise from other residents was definitely unusual. I hurried to the front door to look out of the peephole when passing through the living room I glanced over at the clock on the wall. It was well after ten thirty which meant the alarm next to my bed had long ago turned itself off. The medicine must've put me out cold because it was definitely not like me to ignore alarms, especially since my livelihood revolved around them every day. It at this point that I got a sinking feeling in my stomach, which later I would understand that it represented the unfamiliar direction things had taken a turn for.

Before I could make it to the peephole to look for any signs of the commotion, I heard a continuous, rapid knock from the other side of my own door- a familiar voice in a persistent yet composed manner, was repeating my name.

"Seanna . . . Seanna are you there? Please, I hope you're there and can open the door."

I could always distinguish Ronald Bowen's calm voice even amongst the chatter of other voices, the noise of the equipment and running vehicles at the most chaotic of accident scenes. I've been partnered up with him since I became a paramedic four years ago, in fact, he was my preceptor when my training went mobile outside of the classroom. I found at first that we had little in common other than the fact that he and I were both half English- his other half was Scottish and mine was African American. When I first met him he was forty-two; old enough to be my father because I was twenty-two, yet his own children were half my age. Our trainer/trainee relationship had been pretty good. I looked up to Ronny because he taught me a great deal and his work ethic was superior. By the end of my training, he told me that I had a knack for paramedic work and encouraged me to stay at Cedar Crest. Soon after my training was over I ended up partnering with him because his old shift partner never returned after a back injury he received while they were on a call. It wasn't long after working with Ronny that we both learned more about each other and built a great working relationship. I wouldn't call him a father figure- he'd swear I was calling him old, but Ronny had become like a favorite uncle to me.

By the time I got to the door which was a few seconds later- without checking first, I swung open the door and instantly assessing my situation; me in my t-shirt, cotton pajama bottoms and ruffled hair- Ronny figured out that I overslept. His face quickly went from an expression of concern to one of relief as he exhaled one big breath.

"Ronny I'm so sorry I-.." I began to say as he interrupted my apology by quickly stepping his tall, medium-framed body past mine inside the apartment and then closing and locking the door.

"I'm glad just glad you're alive and okay," he responded, hastily checking the peep-hole in the door and putting the sliding chain on. He was dressed in his uniform, complete with the hospital logo jacket, his stethoscope and the purple-handled bandage scissors we're accustomed to using quite a few times during a shift.

"You know it's not like me to oversleep like that. I guess I was just worn out from all those extra shifts, plus I thought I was coming down with a cold last night." I went on without pausing. It hadn't even registered in my head that he might just call first. Then I thought about the answering machine.

"Oh crap! I bet Barb called me and she's gonna be pissed I didn't answer." I rambled on as I hurried through the medium-sized living room area to the kitchen counter where the answering machine was. Ronny was now speaking in a monotone fashion but I didn't hear a word he said until I saw there wasn't a single message waiting to be heard. Confused at the large red *zero* on the machine, I turned around to look at Ronny, who stood only a few feet from the entryway still. It definitely was not like Barb Goodwin, our Paramedic Operations Supervisor, to not call someone when they were fifteen or thirty minutes late- let alone three-and-a-half hours. If anyone kept perfect time and knew where people should be, it was Barb.

"She hasn't called? What's got her so distracted?" If I was lucky maybe she had an early morning meeting and didn't notice my not showing up.

"Seanna you haven't heard what's going on? Even right outside now there is a total panic. Someone outside was attacking people trying to leave in a car when I was coming in your building. People everywhere are getting attacked." He looked toward the floor as if to reflect on these recent events.

At that instant, he and I both rushed over to the living area, Ronny going directly for the manual switch to the television when I was headed for the remote control on the end table. I don't think the magnitude of the whole incident rang any bells right away- this was until I heard more unfamiliar screams outside. As he turned the television on, I ran to the kitchen window to see the commotion Ronny recently just described to me for the first time, confirming all of what I heard earlier.

My small kitchen window overlooking the parking lot big enough for about twenty-five cars revealed quite a bit of commotion. Several of my neighbors that I knew were carrying hampers and bags, loading them into their cars in a manner reminiscent to those fleeing a hurricane. I imagine in those containers were only the things they cherished and absolutely needed. Things like medications, toothbrushes, deodorant and clothing items- along with diapers and toys if you had children, as was the case for the Mercado family, who was now trying to leave in a hurry. They lived right below me on the first floor and had three small children, all of whom were present outside as their mother Francesca quickly opened the back door to their sedan, placing the youngest into the car seat while the other two climbed in as fast as they could from the same side. The youngest child was crying inconsolably as he was being buckled in. Manuel, their father and husband was at the very back of the car putting items in the trunk when he leaned over and said something to Francesca. Although they were in a hurry, this all seemed normal. I still couldn't understand what all the panic Ronny described was about. He was tuned into the television. I could hear the news anchorman talking. Another couple who lived on the first floor carried fewer personal belongings yet jumped into their hatchback and sped off.

"Can you turn it up a little; I can't hear what they're saying!" I said over my shoulder as I kept an eye on the Mercados. Both Manuel and Francesca were both at the back of the car now loading the rest of the items. They both kept looking over their shoulders every few seconds or so.

"I can't. I'm worried someone might hear the TV. I think they're attracted to noise."

Ronny said in a low tone. "What's attracted to noise?" I replied, probably louder than I should have. In that same moment, a man came into my window view, stumbling slowly. I live on the second floor and he was at least fifty feet from the Mercado's and their sedan but I could see the blood covering most of his clothing from where I was. His face was dull and listless and it didn't even appear that he was focused on any particular thing but he picked up his pace, giving attention to the family right below. I'd seen this look a hundred times before in my line of work but I had to squint to verify my own eyesight. This poor guy had the look of the dying and the dead. Of course in those few seconds I couldn't tell if the blood was his own or someone else's but by the way he was walking, he definitely had some sort of debilitating injury. As I spoke over my shoulder, "Ronny, you gotta see this man, he's hurt pretty bad." Francesca saw this man too and screamed as Manuel gave her a push that indicated 'get in the car'. She took the few quick steps to get to the passenger door as Manuel put the last bag in the trunk, slammed it closed and darted to the driver's seat with keys in hand. The staggering man made it to the back of the car and started reaching for the back window where the children were seated. From where I was I could see the fear in their faces as Manuel turned the ignition on, barely waiting for the engine to turn over before putting it in gear. The car jerked in reaction and skidded off as he had to make a u-turn in order to get out of the lot. The stumbling, injured man stretched forward as if he would go after the car but was distracted by another woman's screams in response to the situation. He then went toward her, more quickly.

"Oh my God, I think that man just tried to attack my neighbors," was all I could mutter from my lips. Ronny got up from the television and came to look out of the window with me. I was a little dumbfounded but Ronny grabbed my arm to divert my attention.

"Seanna, you need to take a look at the TV, here." We walked back through the living room where due to what we just saw outside he went even further to the front door and looked through the peep-hole for a few seconds. What I saw on the TV for those few minutes was an indication that humanity had changed forever. In short, there were two news anchors who regularly broadcasted with the Philadelphia local news station and two other men who were some sort of officials describing a, "Rapidly spreading *pandemic outbreak of epic proportions, affecting countless individuals both locally and throughout the east coast where the origin is assumed to have occurred."* There were also reports of similar incidences in neighboring states, possibly as far away as Chicago and St. Louis but they reiterated several times that they were still unconfirmed. Across the bottom of the screen there was a simultaneous message that read:

"ATTENTION PA RESIDENTS: THERE HAVE BEEN A SERIES OF INCIDENTS IN THIS AREA REQUIRING THE QUARANTINE OF SOME METROPOLITAN AREAS AND THE CONTAINMENT OF INDIVIDUALS DISPLAYING CERTAIN SYMPTOMS— LAW ENFORCEMENT OFFICIALS ARE INSTRUCTING PEOPLE TO REMAIN INDOORS, RESTRICT TRAVEL TO AND FROM THE

COUNTIES AND CITIES LISTED AT THE BOTTOM OF THE SCREEN. OFFICIALS ARE ALSO INSTRUCTING PEOPLE TO CALL 9-1-1 IF YOU WITNESS ANYONE BEING ATTACKED OR DISPLAYING UNUSUAL BEHAVIORS- ESPECIALLY IF THEY HAVE RECENTLY VISITED ANY OF THESE COUNTIES,"

It was definitely a surreal moment whose circumstances hinted only a few moments ago with the events outside my kitchen window and my abrupt awakening before that. Apparently, it had been going on elsewhere since at least yesterday evening because there was footage, some amateur and some professionally taken of obviously dead individuals enraged, chasing and attacking people. Numerous times they had to mention that the images were graphic and warned the viewing public to keep children away from the TV because there was no editing done to the footage we were seeing. They were also giving out information regarding official actions that were being taken by police and military units in order to keep people safe, supposedly to catch the individuals in question and to restore order. Moments later they added that the first reports were contained information about questionable individuals two nights ago outside of Washington D.C and how those individuals couldn't be found and that cause of this outbreak had not yet been determined. Most attempts were unsuccessful at stopping the attack because no one knew what to do. Whole police units were missing and the death toll was estimated to be in the hundreds or thousands by now and those were conservative numbers.

Apparently some officers were successful in taking down the subjects and initial examinations had been done with more tests to follow and yes, a few captured seemingly 'alive' were found to be clinically dead- if that makes any sense that they had no pulse, no blood pressure and their temperatures were warm though not at ninety-eight point six, like standard. The officials being interviewed said they had to be restrained at all times or else all they would do was attack until the targets themselves were dead.

Because I was standing there, absolutely still for as long as they would talk, Ronny decided to remind me of the fact that this affected us too, right now.

"That's about all they've been saying for the last couple of hours, there's really nothing new so far," he spoke in a low tone rather quickly.

"This is all news to me. What's Cedar Crest doing about all of this?" I asked, referring to the hospital that we worked for.

"Well my dear, you managed to clock out right before the start of all the chaos in our neck of the woods. About as soon as you and I got off from our shift together yesterday afternoon, they're thinking that's when we started getting infected patients from this area. The hospital went on full lockdown at three this morning after there were massive reports of injuries downtown overnight. The night shift was overrun with them. The same thing happened too at Muhlenberg who picked up the slack."

I couldn't believe what I was being told. I stayed over till almost seven-thirty because it was Thursday night and since some people like to get the weekend started early, we were expecting there would be a few more calls- hence, my overtime opportunity. Ronny saw me playing out the four hours of my overtime in my head, look-ing for clues but I interrupted him before he could finish.

"I didn't notice anything weird yesterday at the hospital or on the streets, in fact Rachel and I did two transports over to Easton and I was done by seven-thirty, home at eight," I told him, as if that would make it better. I started thinking more specifically at things that went on yesterday because in my mind, there had to be some clues something like this was happening. This is not the movies— for crying out loud! I looked over at the kitchen window as I heard more glass breaking and yelling. What surprised me was the lack of sirens signifying help was on the way.

"Have you talked to Deanna? Are the kids okay?" I asked him. I had spent enough time on my experience with the whole ordeal.

"Yeah she's about as shocked as you are and everyone else. I called her right after I got to Cedar Crest. Luckily the phones were still working. I told her to pack up the basics and leave. I'm going to meet them at her parent's house in Pittston. She thinks it should be safer out there with less people— I agree. They should be there by now. She'll try to call me soon as they get there." He sounded optimistic about the task his wife had to complete on her own. After seeing what the Mercado's just went through— I was a little more worried.

I then had a quick thought about my own folks. My younger brother Junior and parents, Ivy and Jackson Sr. still live in Philadelphia and from what I heard on the news it was pretty bad in that area. My father is from England originally and was in his last year of service with Her Majesty's Armed Forces after graduating from the University of London when he met my mother while she was studying abroad through Rutgers Uni-versity. When I asked her years ago as a child about how and why she ended up 'across the pond' in England, she told me she wasn't up to trying out the few years of French she'd learned in high school and that a year of college in England still seemed exciting, yet a little less foreign than other countries. She always said she was grateful for the opportunity to study there and besides— I should be glad of it because it was the reason my brother and I are here. Her and my father, who I think come from opposite ends of the track— aside from being different races and nationalities, are nev-ertheless a good match for each other because other than their children, they put nothing else above their relationship— plus they are too darn considerate of each other. I'm sure my grandparents on both sides wanted to be sure if they were right for each other. Both had to pass the test of meeting each other's families. Something tells me though if they were anything like they are now, once you see them together, it would be plain heartless not to root for their kind of love. I was told the story of how they met and it was fate. I understood too how, once you see the same person at a few different locations, the mall, the train, local bar and café, over a few weeks you can't help but think they are either stalking you or maybe you should strike up a conversation. My mother was just gorgeous with her smooth, caramel skin tone, naturally long hair and perfect smile. I'm sure my father couldn't help but notice her. When he saw her for the fourth or fifth time— at a library, he approached her after a few casual strolls in passing, struck up a conversation and soon after they hung out a few times. They both were nervous about a biracial relationship because neither one had ever experienced such. The apprehension faded quickly. When my mother's second semester was over she decided she couldn't leave my father without the promise of a future together and my father answered her both verbally and by sending flowers to her parent's home that were delivered by the time she got off the plane and to her home doorstep in Jersey City. My father applied for a visa and was in the U.S. six months later. They soon married and settled in Camden, NJ where his older brother, Lloyd was a doctor already living nearby in Philadelphia and establishing his career in biomedical research. After my mother graduated from Rutgers she got a job working as a communications assistant. Two years later, I was born and three years later, Jackson Jr. was born.

Speaking of my brother, he's neither like my mother or my father. He may have my father's engineering intelligence but he definitely tries to play himself to be cooler than he really is. I don't blame him though, I blame *MTV* and all these reality shows that pressure young guys to act more established and mature than they really are. I swear that boy was probably nineteen before he lost his virginity because he did believe in love. It's just unfortunate that his girlfriend didn't — otherwise she loved quite a few people from my understanding. I met her once, Reyna, she was exotic looking too– just the dark, long haired type that wore too much makeup that attempted to present a woman to the world as a natural beauty– it didn't fool me. I called her 'the girl next door who invited over all the boys' because I went to high school with a few of her type. Her kind are the ones assumed to be the good girls at first sight but they are the worst in the bunch– doing things a way that definitely requires experience. She could play guys several at time and not make a mistake therefore my brother's kind heart and childlike spirit was no match even with his fairly decent looks. He played it cool when they broke up after a year but I'd say Reyna played him like fiddle. The bottom line was they were both freshmen in college and to expect the same thing to happen to two generations in a row is absurd. This was a different age than what our parents lived through in the dating world. There weren't as many distractions and low expectations about long term relationships. I explained this all to him, told him not to get mom and dad's hopes up next time unless he was positive she was 'the one'. In the meantime, I'm sure he went back to his Xbox 360.

I myself, after a couple of mediocre dates landed a relationship– after I put my foot in my mouth, crying that I had given up on relationships and was going to go live in a monastery. Ronny cracked up when he heard me say that during a shift two years ago. It was like the heavens waited until I hit my own version of a relationship rock bottom, at twenty-four, mind you. After one of my lengthy rants in the ambulance or "bus" as we call it, Ronny said I was a just a baby and had to give it time. We both were wrong because by the end of that week Rachel Rory, one of the second shift paramedics– whom I worked with just last night invited me to a party thrown by some graduate students at Lehigh University in neighboring Bethlehem, PA. Although I didn't want to go, I offered to drive so she could at least have a good time without worrying how to get back home, besides it's just a short drive– less than 10 miles. Once we arrived I spent the first hour after casual introductions hiding out in the corner, observing both the familiar and awkward conversations that took place among the dozen or so people in front of me. I'd swear, whereas some people try too hard, Rachel was a natural at picking her targets– getting what she wanted, which was a late night incursion with a decent male prospect without the necessity of a commitment, unless the night was remarkable. It wasn't my most favorite quality about her but she had the courage I did not. I was just accepting the possibility that I might be driving back to Allentown by myself when I was approached by Graham– whom I'd not met before. I remember our conversation being a little awkward at first, something about the rules of the shared rental house being 'no strangers allowed,' which was his cue to get to know me or else he'd have to boot me out. Corny, I know– but it was cute and unexpected and after looking into his attractive, brownish-green eyes and seeing the most perfect set of pearly whites in a long time, I couldn't help but go along with the storyline. Long story short; neither myself or Rachel went home that evening. Graham and I stayed up until sunrise– talking, after which we both slept on separate couches. Rachel on the other hand, did get lucky but as usual it was one of many firsts and lasts.

Graham turned out to be just perfect for me. I kept thinking that dating him was too good to be true which made me suspicious when I didn't need to be. I've never been close to being called ugly–or chasing the men away but Graham was good look-ing and friendly enough to where other female students at his school would inquire and that was as far as it went. I had my doubts in the very beginning, but they were just that– the normal insecurities every woman has; that it would be possible for Graham to get closer to one of the other female PhD candidates because they might have more in common academically and maybe there was a better future with someone he was already able to spend more time with.

I must've been in a daze thinking about them all and listening to all this stuff going on because Ronny interrupted me, "I came by to see if you were okay. I hadn't heard from you since we worked yesterday and when you didn't show up for the shift this morning I thought. . . anyways, you should try your phone and see if you can get in touch with your folks and Graham. The lines are going in and out right now. I don't think they'll be around much longer."

"What about cell . . ." I started to say but he cut me off by saying the reception was funny now especially after the switch to the emergency system. I grabbed the house phone from the counter almost dropping it as I started dialing the two-one-five Philadelphia area code. Again, glass shattered followed by two gunshots outside. Instinc-tively, I ducked behind the counter, almost knocking over one of the barstool chairs while dialing the rest of the numbers. The phone rang five times before I was surprised and then disappointed by the answering machine picking up. I know I've called the number a thousand times over the years with the message changing only once or twice because of my brother and I moved out and the resulting enthusiastic, *'Hello,*

you've reached the emptynesters who are out on vacation or having a wild party of
their own after all these years so please leave a message and we'll get back to you!

It seemed like an eternity listening to it this time.

"Hello . . . Mom . . . Dad . . . please, pick up. I've seen the news and I hear things
are pretty bad everywhere. I don't know what's going on . . . I'm okay . . . Ronny is
here checking on me, God I hope you all are alright . . . Umm . . . Please just stay
inside and I'll try to see if I can get there if they're allowing people into the city. I'm
gonna call Junior and see if he's okay– I hope he's with you. I love you guys and I'll try
calling again soon . . . Bye."

I didn't know what else to say.

As I stood up from the safety of the floor and counter space I looked at Ronny who
was also checking his pager. "Nothing yet," He said, answering my unspoken question.

"It doesn't mean your parents are in danger." He added.

"Okay, and it doesn't mean Deanna and the kids are in danger either." I shot right
back, trying to sound as confident as possible about his situation. I picked up the phone
again as I heard sirens this time that sounded like an ambulance. I was intent on making as many phone calls as possible because I knew Ronny was right, I probably only
had a limited time before the phones would be a privilege, if at all. With the dial tone
there, I started dialing my brother's cell phone number and it immediately went to
voicemail which meant that his phone was probably powered off. I didn't leave a message figuring he'd see the missed call. I hung up immediately to dial Graham's number
and to my surprise there was an answer. His voice was everything I needed to hear–
to start crying. I turned into an emotional mess in an instant.

"Seanna . . . Baby I'm so glad to hear your voice. The phones are in and out. Are
you okay? Listen, don't go outside! I tried to call you a few times this morning but our
phones on campus were limited to emergency calls only, then they went out altogether
. . . Some weird shit is going down– dead people roaming around and attacking the
living, it's unbelievable!" Graham spoke calmly always but this chatter took a moment
to get adjusted to– I was processing every detail because everything he's gone through
was another perspective of the absolute truth. The only others I've witnessed at this
point were what I heard from Ronny, the television and what I saw earlier with the
neighbors. I was trying to picture people– dead but moving around, in the little quiet
town of Bethlehem, Allentown and elsewhere.

"Sea . . . Sea . . . Babe, can you hear me?" He asked me after he heard a lack of
response from me.

"Yes, are you alright? I need to get to you, and see about my parents and Junior. I
think it's bad here too, I don't want to stay here and I haven't heard from anyone except Ronny who's here now. Philly is bad according to the news– they're telling
everyone to stay away. Ronny needs to get to his wife and kids. I'm getting scared
Graham." I rushed everything because I knew he'd get it.

"Bethlehem is not far out of the way home." I said quickly. I could get there and
we can head to Philly in no time.

"You shouldn't leave your apartment, Seanna. Darin got into it with one of those-infected people. He got some blood in his eyes and mouth and quite a few scratches, before he was okay but now he's upstairs bedridden, not even able to talk anymore. His temperature is up. There's some kind of a fever it causes." Graham went silent.

"Is Chad there too?" I asked of his other roommate. I wouldn't want Graham to be alone there to deal with Darin and keep out of harms way.

"Yeah, he's up there with him now. I don't know what we're going to do since the hospital is not an option anymore. If he gets worse . . . "

"Okay, okay don't think about that just yet. The news said to call the number on the screen and make a report," I said, trying to recall the broadcasted instructions while squinting at the television screen to see the number at the bottom.

I was thinking of anything that could help but I was coming up short for advice. Paramedics rely on a well designed network of communication and equipment along with other professionals for scenarios that we've been trained to handle. There was nothing in the books for this one.

"I don't think you should stay there," I said boldly. "I want to see if my car is still in the lot. If it's safe I can be there in twenty minutes tops. I can take a look at Darin and see if anything can be done. He probably needs to be at the hospital. Try and keep him cool," I said. That sounded reasonable to me.

"Sea, I- . . ." He started but then there was a click and then silence. I looked at the phone receiver, which was stupid- I know, it was obvious the phones were out again as he described earlier.

"I've got to get to him," I said as I hung the phone up and hurried past Ronny to get to my bedroom to change clothes and pack a few items. I grabbed my large back-pack from the corner- it was a gift I got from Graham as a one month anniversary present after learning my occupation and then how I was always carrying multiple bags out the door during the times he saw me off to work. It would serve its purpose well today. I threw it on the bed and went to the dresser grabbing a few essential items- throwing them at the backpack. Socks, underwear, a few t-shirts, my not-for-yoga pants- because they were less bulky and were reasonably appropriate still for May weather, deodorant and a few treasures I had on my dresser such as the five by nine framed photos of me with my parents and brother taken a little over a year ago when we all went on vacation together to the Grand Canyon and then to Las Vegas, at the request of my brother for his twenty-first birthday. The other photo was of me and Graham in a classic PG-rated lover's pose; us facing the camera with him hugging me from behind. I remember the day the photo was taken by Darin. The three of us were in Center City- Downtown Allentown, at a bistro. We were waiting for Chad and his girlfriend to show up for lunch. It was early last fall, the perennial flowers in the garden space in between two buildings had almost finished blooming for the year and Darin was always on top of photo opportunities with his iPhone. It turned out nicer than I thought because I was not nearly photo ready- it took a five minute bathroom pit stop for a makeup and clothing adjustment. I do remember thinking that the flowers would be in the photo too but it was a close up and the light was great because the sun was high allowing the sunlight to shine into the space. The flowers ended up being 'mood enhancers for the moment' according to Darin. Today I would use some of those photographs to help search for my family, if needed.

I quickly changed out of the clothes I slept peacefully in, putting on a bra first before taking off the t-shirt because the bedroom door was wide open. My most comfortable pair of jeans and a cotton three-quarter sleeve shirt were folded in a chair nearby along with other laundry because I hadn't yet put them away. I grabbed the items, took off my bottoms and threw them on along with my socks and tennis shoes. Ronny appeared at the doorway just as I was finished dressing and shoving the rest of my selected items into the backpack— watching my frantic motions, my hesitations, and my reflecting on the memories associated with the photos.

"I'm not so sure your going to Bethlehem is a good idea, Seanna," he calmly phrased.

"Yeah, well what would you do Ronny? You're about to head off to catch up with your family and that risk is okay with you? I can't just sit here," I said without breaking my movements.

I heard more screaming outside and another round of gunshots— which made me stop. I knew looking out of the window might allow me to see another attack on someone else's life and that was too much for me to handle right now. I'd seen a lot of damage done to the human body; mangled bones bent and broken under stress they were never meant to handle. I've seen a person nearly emptied of their blood, bowels and other organic contents— complete with smells. I've seen some miracles too where individuals have been on the brink of being pronounced dead but in a last attempt to restart the heart— a shot of epinephrine with multiple uses of a defibrillator where the still monitors roar back to life. I've also seen victims of drownings that were probably under water for ten or twenty minutes brought back due to persistent forced oxygen techniques — correctly done CPR. Everyone in my line of work understands that without medical intervention in these circumstances, death is absolute and there is no re-animation. The stuff happening now was off the books.

"I know it won't make a difference but can I ask you to just think for a minute. What if your parents call back? Landlines are more dependable than cell phones— you know that. What if they're on their way here? You've seen the TV— the bigger cities are worse than here. You'd be heading right into trouble, Seanna." He looked me square in the eyes. I caught his glance and exhaled a heavy sigh.

I heard Ronny's point and I know I didn't have time to debate this with him. I knew he was at least partially right but there was no partial way to go about staying alive. What if I got outside only to find that my poor little Ford Escape had been stolen or disabled? I doubt I would make it back upstairs into my apartment without becoming one of the next loud voices or ruckus heard now once every few minutes. What if I got as far as Philadelphia to my parent's house only to be overtaken by these walking, expired souls? Do any of the methods work for killing them, again, permanently that we've seen in the movies? Now I really wish I had bought the *Zombie Survival Guide* I saw on the bookstand during one of my many trips to *Target*. I'd bet there was some useful advice which could help us out now.

"Ronny, you know your advice is like gold to me but think about it, I haven't heard from my parents or my brother. Graham is the only person aside from you that I've have talked to and I think it would be better if I got to him and we both together figure out a next step– be it going into the city or away from it."

I was on the edge of another round of tears. Every moment I didn't hear from my family was a step further into the unknown and I wasn't prepared to think about all the things that might've already happened to them. Picking up my nearly full backpack, I took a few steps around Ronny out of my bedroom and into the bathroom. Once there, I grabbed a fresh washcloth and a few other toiletries. Within seconds I was back out into the narrow hallway where inside a tiny closet I kept a firstaid kit. It was basic with gauze, compresses, bandages, and aspirin, etc. – upgraded with a few supplies that were from the hospital but were expired and therefore could no longer be used for patient care according to hospital policy. It was in its own separate little gym bag and ready to go.

I raised the firstaid bag , which Ronny had seen before, "Do you think the pharmacy is still open?" I said jokingly as I returned to the living room. I didn't expect it but he smirked and returned with, "I wish I'd thought about it while I was at the hospital earlier. It's all messed up there now– you couldn't imagine the chaos when it all fell apart. The last thing I was thinking about was staying there– let alone getting anything. I've never abandoned a job before . . .   Not even in the military during combat med-evacs. There were just too many of them. They tried to lock things up to keep people safe but whoever wasn't infected pretty much tore things down trying to get to safety."

I knew this would bother him for longer than he would ever admit. Apparently, these were desperate times that didn't have an end in sight. The TV was still on the major news network now with captions at the bottom saying in quotations *"As many as hundreds of thousands may be affected."*

CHAPTER TWO

I couldn't move. It wasn't my first day on the job yet all I could do after arriving at the scene of an accident involving three cars– initially caused by a deer crossing a two-lane section of highway, was to stand there horrified at what I saw. Two teens were ejected from the first car which was subsequently hit by the car behind them– who was then hit by a van in an unsuccessful attempt to avoid the mess. The fog was brutal that morning. Those two teens were now twenty feet or so away from the rear ended sedan whose make and model could only be identified from the front portion of the car. Ronny and I were second to arrive on the scene, only minutes after the state patrol–lights and sirens in full. It was immediately clear who we could help and who was beyond our aid. The passenger of the second car was unable to move without help while the driver luckily was able to call police from his cell phone. The third driver, a man in his thirties stood next to his van almost overcome with shock. The two teens, both male, lay on the highway motionless with obvious impact wounds from the initial contact with the windshield and subsequent contact with the paved road. I knew after Ronny and the patrolman ran over to officially pronounce them that my job was to care for the next most critical, to stabilize them and alert dispatch of our estimated arrival time to Cedar Crest or a closer hospital based on the patient's condition.

"Let's move!" Ronny said as he went around me to grab the stretcher with both hands and it sprang into movement. "Sir, are you okay? We're going to help the person still in the car over there but I want you to keep breathing and alert the patrolman over there if anything changes. Another ambulance is just a few minutes out . . . Sean-na, let's go!"

"Seanna, you shouldn't go out alone. You haven't seen what's out there like I have. It's bad. You'll never be able to make it by yourself." Ronny stood between me the front door now. If I didn't know better, it would seem like he was going to block me from leaving.

I wasn't much of an actress and I never signed up for the debate team during my years in school so it was going to take some pretty good word play in order to get Mr. Bowen here to agree with the actions I was about to take. If he was anything like Jackson Sr., my father whom I was never able to get anything past, I'd be staying right here until this thing blew over, even if it meant I would be the only one left with a pulse.

"Ronny, please look at it from my point of view. What if Deanna hadn't heard from you? Don't tell me that she'd sit there for even a second without coming to see about you. I can't wait for the phones to start working nor can I wait on someone to get here to me." I turned to look at the television because again I was sure the tears would start up. I could already see my vision getting blurry but it cleared again almost instantly as my focus shifted to the live video feeds from various cities such as New York, Atlantic City, New Jersey and Philadelphia– all of which told the same story of massive infection rates, attacks, rioting, fires, and almost a complete breakdown of civility. There were eyewitness accounts given by people who witnessed attacks carried out by, "obviously dead persons who have reanimated." They quickly added that as a result there were also many unintentional deaths. These deaths where because people assumed some-one was infected and were killed over what was more or less the similar behavior as-sociated with being in shock; incoherent, unresponsive, etc. It was clear at this point some people were not taking any chances. The news panel members were careful in reporting what used to be unbelievable but was now undeniable fact. With the exception of the live video feeds it would be a challenge to even the most talented Hollywood graphic effects artist to recreate.

If there was any chance of me sticking around my apartment longer due to safety reasons, it might have been now. The violence seen on television and right outside seemed to be almost war–like in nature with the mounting reports of attacks and kill-ings in self–defense. Not to mention seeing some of the landmarks in Philadelphia that I grew up around now burning to the ground. For a brief moment I'm sure the camera-man showed scenes of the corner store I used to go to most days after school now being looted. This brought another important subject up in my mind: protection.

"So how are people stopping them?" I asked Ronny. He knew exactly whom I was referring to.

"I had to . . . It's just like the movies. If you penetrate a good portion of the skull to the brain tissue– they seem to stop for good. Even then, the more damage– the better." Ronny looked at me dead–serious, no pun intended, to make sure I understood. "Noth-ing else counts." He added quickly.

"Okay. Just like the movies." I nodded.

I couldn't think of anything that I owned that might be effective enough to expose brain tissue other than the solid wood baseball bat I used a few years ago when Rachel and I played softball during the summer for Alley Champ's bar league. As a paramedic I wasn't used to thinking about how to expose brain matter. If anything, I was to protect it from further damage. I grabbed the bat from the closet out of the corner it was in, kicking the baseball glove I'd placed on the handle as it rolled out onto the floor. Ronny seemed to approve of it.

"That's no gun but it'll stop one of them if you do it right. Just don't get two of them at once." He advised.

"I have a pretty decent swing– I'll make it work until I can get something better." I took the handle gripping it with both of my hands and then sat it next to my slowly growing pile of essentials. I turned next to go into the kitchen so I could get my note pad and pen that was normally used for grocery lists. I wrote as quickly as I could the best thing I could think of:

Left here at 1100 going to Graham's

I'll keep checking the phones and trying to call everyone whenever possible.

I'm safe and okay.

I may try to get to Philly as soon as possible.

–Seanna

I thought it was good enough since I had no clue who, if anyone, would read it next. I placed the note square on the coffee table where I was sure someone would see it. We heard a loud explosion–like sound which shook the whole building. It appeared to come from the parking lot and I could see the dark smoke blowing westward past my kitchen window. A few seconds later Ronny's pager went off. I looked at him for some confirmation of good news because after that moment I was sure we both needed some right now.

"It's Deanna's folks' number." He said with a look of relief. I was definitely glad for him. Similar to everyone, his wife and kids were his life. This was the best news either of us heard all morning.

"I guess that means some of the roads are still safe– you better get on your way before it's too late." I said, feeling more optimistic now myself for both of us and our travels. The smoke still flowing outside caught my glance, I could smell it now as well. Ronny walked over to the counter where the note pad was and started jotting down a few things. As soon as he finished he handed it to me.

"What's this?" I said as I accepted it from him.

"It's the address to Deanna's parents. Their phone number is there too in case the phones are ever stable enough." He reached over to the phone, picked it up to check for a dial tone and hung it back up to no avail. "They are still out. It's luck how I even got the page. Seanna, you're welcome to come up there whenever you see necessary since I can tell I won't be able to convince you to go now."

"Thanks but you all won't have room for me too, let alone anyone I bring with me." I told him.

"I've told you before about that place– it's in the middle of nowhere and I promise you, they've got plenty. It's right near Scranton; four–seventy–six to eighty–one to the Pittston exit. Please, just remember it as an option okay? Try to get in touch with us if you can because I'll be worried about you all until I hear anything." I think he could tell that we were running out of time here.

"The first mail truck I see headed to Scranton . . ." I said dryly. As if there were nothing more to say, I grabbed my backpack, first aid bag, purse and baseball bat. Ronny grabbed the first aid bag from my arm— freeing up one hand. I'm guessing the idea of self defense by lethal means for me had not yet resonated into actual preparation. My heart was fluttering in response to the sudden movement and adrenaline increase. I started breathing deeply and looking to Ronny for his lead. I didn't notice until now the shorter version of a night stick that was apparently hidden by his jacket. He grabbed the stick with one hand and before opening the door he again briefed me concerning the nature of what it was we were dealing with.

"They're not all that fast. You can probably get away by running from them but don't get yourself cornered. They'll bite, scratch and tear you up in no time. From what I've seen, either way will end in infection. Watch out for their blood spatter and whatnot." He paused to let it all sink in.

It was as quick of a lesson I'd probably ever received for anything. It wasn't like learning to ride a bike where if you fell you simply got back on and the most you'd have was scraped knee. Ronny was telling me something that meant the difference from being actually alive or becoming a killer myself after a sufferable death. I'd like to wake myself up because it seemed like a nightmare. Like the poker players would say, I guess this meant we were "all in," no going back and definitely no second chances.

"Okay, I got it." I took another deep breath. "My car is parked around the back on the side." Ronny had come and picked me up a few times for work when Graham borrowed my SUV so he knew the layout of the building and parking lot. Ronny said he'd get us to my car and I would then drop him off at his. I was now focused on what might be on the other side of the door.

Seemingly like something out of an action movie, Ronny checked the narrow perspective of the peephole one last time, nodded his head and opened the door. He checked both directions and slowly walked out of the doorway, motioning for me to follow. The apartment building had an elevator in the front and stairs in the back to which we were headed. My apartment was on the second floor, yet closer to the front of the building. On a good day it would take me less than a minute to get to the back because there were just six apartments on each floor. The elevator, when not in use, took only seconds longer but now those extra seconds made a difference. As we quietly crept down the hallway past the one apartment and then the next, I heard crying from an adjacent apartment. The apartment belonged to a friendly, older lady named Ruth Leonard. I always called her Ruthie. I was sure it was her who was in distress. Ruthie was eighty-four and still very independent. I automatically stopped in front of her door.

Without hesitation, I started knocking on her door quietly and calling her name similar to the way Ronny did for me, hoping it wouldn't catch anyone's attention but hers. As expected for someone her age, her hearing abilities were past their prime which sometimes made casual conversation a little difficult. Ronny heard the noise. I could see his disapproval. He went on and checked around the corner of the hallway- just where the back door was and quickly came back toward me.

"What are you doing?" He said as loudly as he could at a whisper.

"I can't just leave my neighbor, what if she's hurt?" I knew this was risky but she was no stranger to me. I gave him with a 'what would *you* do?' expression. Ronny leaned into the door to listen for any commotion.

Just then, the handle turned with a little difficulty. After a few seconds the lock was turned, the door knob turned again and the door opened slowly. Thinking he heard a noise, Ronny went and looked around the corner again to make sure no one was coming and hurried back to Ruthie's apartment just as she opened the door.

"Aww, Ruthie," was all I could whisper. At a glance, she was a small but spry woman who was no more than five feet tall. She now stood in front of me in her nightgown which was saturated with blood and I couldn't tell if the blood was hers. Surprised, Ronny and I both quickly stepped inside her apartment. After Ruthie told us she was alone, he locked the door.

"Double your gloves," Ronny said, pulling two pair of latex gloves from his pocket and sliding them on. I quickly went in my first aid bag and did the same.

"Ruthie, tell me what happened to you," I said as I helped her sit in her easy chair. She was a bit shaken up but I was going to be patient enough to wait for her response.

"I woke up a little while ago after I heard commotion outside. I went downstairs to get the newspaper and to see what was going on when this strange man came by the door– he looked like he needed help or something, I don't know. When he saw me he started pushing at the door and he came after me!" She started to cry. "I'm just an old woman, what could I have that he wants? He started grabbing at me and biting like some animal. He was bleeding and it got all over me, see?" Ruthie showed me her gown and I let out a sigh of relief because it sounded like it was not hers. This was not enough for Ronny though and he gently checked around her and asked her if she had any cuts from the attack.

"No, sir I don't. But he did bite me a little through my housecoat– see, right here." Ruthie pulled up the sleeve from her left arm and on her forearm there were the markings that looked like teeth impressions that had broken the skin and bled. There was also some bruising and a little yellow mucous around the site. The bruising itself was much larger than the teeth marks.

"Damn." I said quietly. Ruthie looked at me with fear in her eyes.

"Can you take me to your hospital Seanna? I don't know when my last tetanus shot was but I don't think I need any stitches. Do you think its okay?"

I was at a loss for words now. I knew without a doubt that I was looking at another victim of all the deadly disorder outside. For the last thirty minutes I'd only seen it from a distance and from the safety of my apartment on the news broadcast. Now, I was right next to someone who's affected– sharing a space and I'll tell you, it was uncomfortable to say the very least. Something inside of me now felt extremely uneasy. It was likely because this was all unfamiliar and overwhelming and most significantly, there was nothing I could do. I looked to Ronny was assessing the situation.

"Ruth, how are you feeling?" he asked as he felt her head for a temperature. He then felt around the bite wound and commented on how it seemed tender and the area was warmer, indicating an infection was present.

"I feel a little dizzy. My head and my arm hurts, probably from the fight. Seanna, do you think you could get me in with that nice doctor- what was his name? He was very nice and attractive too- he was a little older than you and single too, doctor- . . . " Ruth stumbled a little now with her speech.

"It was Dr. Erickson, and yes he is nice." *And probably dead now*, I thought to my-self. I stood and walked to Ruthie's kitchen counter where a single glass was. It looked clean. I went to the sink and filled it with cool water and brought it back to her. Ronny took me to the side of the living room where we could talk in private.

"I'm sure she's got the infection and at her age it won't take long to . . . take over." He slowed as he was trying his best to be sensitive about it.

"What are we gonna do?" I asked him, although I already knew the answer, at least in part.

"She won't be able to come with us because I don't think it'll be safe for her- or us. I have an idea though." He got up and went back to Ruthie and asked her where she kept her medications and then disappeared into the bathroom, where they were kept, I assume. He came back after a short time with one pill bottle and a box of *Uni-som* in hand. The pill bottle was *Pramipexole* for Restless Leg Syndrome. He opened it and took out two pills and one tablet of the sleep aid.

"Ruthie, I'm going to give you some of your medications that you have already, because I think they will help you until we can get you to the hospital, they will help you to relax until we can get a hold of Dr Erickson." Ronny said as he handed them to her with the glass of water. He looked at me suggesting that I play along. I threw in few words.

"Yeah, Ruthie he's right. The phones are out right now but until they can get them fixed we are going to have to wait with you- and it will make you feel better." I said as I looked at her arm again and it was slightly worse than before. In that small amount of time the bruising had spread to just above her tiny wrist. I could tell too that Ruthie was beginning to get anxious now as she was becoming a little fidgety. Ruthie reluc-tantly took the pills while I went to look for another gown in her bedroom- which was just about as dainty as you can imagine for a woman of her time. I wanted to replace her blood soaked gown to at least give her the dignity she deserved in her last hours. Speaking of, I didn't know exactly how she would go, maybe Ronny had seen people die at the hospital and then after a short time return to life in an altered state causing them to harm others, who would then die- only to do the same thing.

I was able to find another night gown. Luckily, most women tend to keep their un-derwear and pajamas in the first few drawers of their dresser. I returned in less than a few minutes only to see that she was looking sickly, her skin was more pale now and she was sweating. Ronny went to the bathroom to get a wash cloth and with cold water he dabbed her forehead. I managed to change her gown with little difficulty- only being cautious of the blood on her gown. Once that was done, we waited. Ruthie began to close her eyes after mumbling a few words.

If I had forgotten about the chaos outside I was reminded quickly as four gunshots were fired.

Ronny broke the silence between us after a few seconds.

"We should get her to bed. I imagine she'll sleep for a while. Hopefully it'll happen then. We need to get going still." He mumbled quietly.

I gently woke Ruthie up, insisting she'd be more comfortable in her bed. She didn't argue as she'd told me before of her nightly routine–taking her pills in the living room, dozing off while watching the evening news, waking up a short time later, and wandering into her bedroom finally. This was what she'd done nearly every day since her husband Albert passed away four years ago. She had no children and only distant relatives she would chat with, on occasion. Any associations she had here in Allentown were likely dealing with crises of their own.

I helped Ruthie up from the chair noting her warmer temperature, got her into bed and told her that Ronny and I would be in the living room trying the phone to see about an ambulance to get to Cedar Crest. Ruthie thanked me for helping her and I told her she was a wonderful neighbor to have. It was only another minute or two after that she was sleeping peacefully again. I didn't want to leave her side but I knew we had to. Our last minutes together as gentle and as simple as this. I would guess now that maybe the next time she woke up– it would be in our best interest to not be around.

I closed the door quietly as I left Ruthie's room.

"She's sleeping now," I confirmed to Ronny who was looking out of the window.

"We should go now," he said as he grabbed my first aid bag. I scanned around the room for Ruthie's keys. They were on a special hook. I assumed that it would be safer if we locked the door behind us when we left. I grabbed my purse, backpack, and baseball bat and glanced down the hallway where Ruthie slept one last time.

"We did what we could under the circumstances and at least the last person she saw was you, her neighbor and friend." He added as he pat my shoulder. He'd probably go on and say a few nice words about her since he met her as well but time was pressing and it seemed the distance to my car could be as long as it wanted to, given the circumstances.

Without further pause he again checked the peephole and opened the door. I closed and locked the door quickly following Ronny the short distance to the hallway back door. I held my keys tightly in my hand because my vehicle was parked close enough to the building where it would be best to spend the time starting the car and driving off versus, fumbling around in a purse and making time to get attacked. Ronny opened the back door into the stairwell and turned to me quickly signaling me to be as quiet as possible. I could hear some noise toward the bottom of the stairwell but I couldn't see anyone from where I was standing. Instead of going into the stairwell Ronny closed the door again as quietly as he could.

"There's one on the first floor by the door," he whispered. The way he said it, I knew he wasn't describing a live person.

"Can we sneak past them?" I whispered back, although I was aware of the obvious danger. He nodded 'no' in response. I thought about turning around and going down the front using the elevators– sure it would take a little more time but it would be worth it if there wasn't one or more of those things wandering around on that end.

"I think this is our best bet for now, get ready to swing." Ronny grabbed his night-stick after securing the first aid bag over his head and shoulder. He then opened the door and we both slowly descended down the stairwell. The stairs were pretty sturdy so we didn't make much noise. I wasn't sure if Ronny was going charge the individual or wait for them to begin to attack us first. The hallway was small enough to where it would be easy to sense someone coming in my opinion so in anticipation, I held my hands around my baseball bat tight until my hands were nearly drained of all blood. In a few steps and a lean over the railing to take a look– we were less than ten feet from what I could see was only one man, his backside to us, dead but moving. Oddly enough, I could also smell him now. The sight and smell of dead flesh reanimated is a kick to one's senses. I knew we were being stealthy enough to where even the Navy SEALS would be proud– but just as instinct leads predator to its prey, he automatically turned to us and let out a groan.

As if to serve a purpose the man, individual, or thing rushed after not Ronny, but *me*. He attempted to come around Ronny and lunge right at my face. I don't know if it was because I was the weaker prey or if he was still into women or whatever but I would swear that he had made a choice– and that choice was me. Ronny took the man by his arm, swung him around until he forced the dead man to land violently with his backside on the stair. I had no choice but to jump backward which caused me to trip backward up the stairs. I scraped the palm of my hand on the concrete face of the stairs making it about half way up– dropping my bat and keys in the process. All I could do was to look on in shock. I couldn't recognize the dead man, aside from the extent of his wounds. One of his eyes were swollen causing it to bulge out of his head, he had a long gash extending from the side of his face and neck to his shoulder. His hair was matted with blood possibly from various other head traumas. The smell was unbelievable now as he was just inches from me. It was not unlike rotted meat mixed with clay or *Playdoh*.

Ronny may have knocked him off of his course but the dead man didn't lose his any of his determination. Without any reaction of pain he turned over onto his belly and began reaching for my legs and groaning at the same time. Ronny hit him on the back of his already bloodied head, exposing more skull– however this only slowed him slight-ly. The dead man kept reaching and grabbing while I tried to kick my legs both defen-sively and as a moving target. I feared what might happen if he caught a good grip. My purse and backpack seemed only to be helpful in keeping me from getting further up the stairs as my arms flailed about in the loose straps of them both. It took both of Ronny's hands on the nightstick drawn over his own head and a final plunge down on the man's head before Ronny forced enough blood and tissue out and the dead man's assault ceased.

I stared at the now again departed, dead man for a few seconds. Part of me was too afraid to move even with the continual flow of blood coming from his head. It took Ronny about half of the time to regain his composure before he realized that we weren't yet finished with our task. He reached out, grabbed my arm and I could feel his strength as he basically hoisted me quickly over the man whose blood now began to cover the bottom four stairs.

"I told you they're something," he said as he leaned over the man and picked up my keys and bat and handed them to me.

"Why'd he come after *me*?" I asked as I tried to catch my breath. "Did you see how he came around you? It was like you weren't even there . . . but I do thank you," Ronny knew not to take it personal– it was a valid question.

"*Please* don't drop your keys again," he said nonchalantly. I'm sure that would've annoyed me, too.

Because I'm sure I couldn't handle it, Ronny again was the one who opened the door leading outside and to both of our surprises, there appeared to be nothing in sight. Mind you, my car was still around the building's corner, not having to come out swinging made a difference. By now my adrenaline was revving up again and it made me shiver noticeably. We both stepped out and turned right, heading to the building's edge where Ronny peeked around the corner. He leaned back quickly to tell me what to expect.

"There are two of them but they are wandering away from your car," he reported quickly.

"Okay, I'm ready."

"If we are quiet enough we should be able to make it without their noticing– I'm parked right on the street in the front. Seanna, please,–"

"I know– I've got the keys." I interrupted him.

Like I had something to prove or some other idiotic explanation, I jumped out in front of him with my keys in hand, spotted the wandering two as he described and took off– jogging as quietly as possible. Ronny was easily right behind me, his long legs keeping up with my quickened pace. My vehicle was about thirty feet from where I was at the time. It was noticeably dented on the passenger side and I could see some wider smears of blood over the dents as well. As I was running, I thought to myself that as long as it was drivable I wasn't about to worry about anything else. I unlocked the doors using the remote control. Ronny was right at my heels and almost passed me until we made it to the car. We both opened the doors at the same time and of course, the combined effort made enough noise for us to be noticed by the two dead ones wandering nearby. They both turned to face us and came stumbling our way– quickly. It would take only a few seconds and I now understood firsthand what my neighbors, the Mercados went through earlier when I watched from the safety of my kitchen window.

I was horrified as I yelled they were coming and Ronny got into his seat, throwing my bag into the backseat. I on the other hand, had a few more items to juggle with as I tried to take off the backpack and purse and slip into the front seat, simultaneously. Ronny grabbed all of the items and I was able to close my front door about a second before the dead two got to my window. I locked the door and quickly put my keys into the ignition as they clawed and pounded at my window. I didn't want to look at them up close and see the disfiguring trauma that most likely caused their deaths. It wasn't possible to know if they knew each other before all of this happened. All I knew was that they were working together to get at us. As soon as the engine came to life I put the vehicle in drive and hit the gas. The dead couple soon disappeared from the side leaving a bloody mucous smudge on my window and a slight hairline crack on the top corner of my door side window from their efforts. It was only another two hundred feet or so to get to Ronny's pickup truck.

"Do you have your keys, now?" I asked him. I was franticly looking around for more of them nearby. If I needed to double back to buy time, I would.

"I'm good to go. Remember what I said earlier, you're more than welcome there." He said as I came to an abrupt stop next to his truck and hit the 'unlock' switch for the door.

"I know you want to check up on your folks but please, be careful, Seanna." He leaned over and kissed my forehead quickly before exiting.

"You too, thanks for coming to check up on me. I may end up heading out your way with my family once I track them down. Hug Deanna and the kids for me." He nodded his head, accepting my decision, got out of my car and quickly jumped into his pickup truck. It started right up and I gave him a 'thumbs up' signal. He nodded again and I took off, making a U-turn right away. He headed eastward and I went westward. Though Allentown was notoriously quiet, as of this morning, it was an entirely different scene than what anyone was used to seeing. More than one burning car was abandoned on the street Graham and I used to take walks on. The only people now walking down the street were the dead-ones; the bodies no longer interested in keeping the town or its remaining live population safe. It was a fitting term and definition for them. I was confident it would stick with me as the description of them forever.

As of now, I wasn't completely confident with any answer regarding whether or not I'd see Ronny Bowen ever again.

CHAPTER THREE

A drive that I've made at least a hundred times over the last two years which ordinarily took less than 15 minutes, curb to curb. From the day's events I could assume might've taken much longer or been a lot shorter depending on where I would finally stop. Voluntarily, I would end up at Graham's doorstep and into his reassuring arms where at least I'd be with one person I love. Both involuntarily and a highly likely option it seemed, I could also end up in a ditch or t-boned at an inter-section. After Ronny and I parted ways I learned right away that traffic laws were no longer obeyed. From now on, all of the lights stood for 'Get there the best way you can'. Ronny and I were not the last ones alive in the area because there were quite a bit of cars and trucks moving, all of them in a hurry.

There were several people running around on the streets and I had the misfortune of seeing just how vicious the dead ones could be. It didn't take long before a young man no older than twenty, while running away from danger, he turned a corner and ran directly into it. I saw him get grabbed and similar to my own experience the dead one went right for the vascular area of the neck. This attack was a success for the dead. Aside from the blood gushing out of the young man's neck I saw how such an attack provides such distraction along with the obvious pain. The poor young man had no time to fight off being eaten alive because he was too consumed with the massive bleeding from his neck. While the young man was down, those few seconds provided enough time for a few dead others to join in and they just started grabbing and biting wherever they could. His fingers, hands, legs and stomach all became a palatable experience for the now growing number of them.

After being honked at, I hit the gas pedal, driving as safely as I could to avoid any cross traffic in the intersection. There was no time now to reflect on the unfortunate event I'd just seen— only thoughts about the next few miles of my journey to what I considered to be the next safe place. Any other day I had taken the same roads running errands, going to and from work, riding around in the ambulance going to and from calls. It seemed so mundane then. Now everything seemed so unfamiliar and so out of my hands as if I'd never been on this road before. Speaking of, I also discovered quickly that I should take the side streets and avoid the main avenues because there was lots of congestion causing more noise due to honking and yelling out of the cars. This seemed to catch the attention of any dead ones nearby in the area. From my estimates there were dozens on this avenue alone. While the cars were stopped for whatever reason the dead ones would attempt to get at the occupants of whatever vehicle was closest. I had a direct view where I could see one of the dead was able to break the window of a car and started attacking the driver and causing the rest of the passengers to flee. Of course, this made them vulnerable to get attacked while at the same time attracting more dead ones. I would judge my distance from the commotion to be at least four hundred feet but I could hear very well the screams and failed pleas to stop. The dead ones had no reserves either on who they would attack. Children, disabled, and the elderly like Ruthie made for even easier targets– which was incredibly sad because if you tried to stop them, you were voluntarily giving up your own life as well. I saw several people's lives end this way on the street that I and the rest of the population in Allentown drove on so many times before.

There were many injured people along the way. It was easier to tell the difference between them and the dead because you could see they were in pain or, at least in shock. In my short observations I saw that the dead ones could be missing an arm or have a foot long gash and not pay the least bit of attention to it. I noticed too that they were disabled only due to the physiological limitations but were not bothered by the sensation of pain. The paramedic in me wanted badly to pull over and help someone but I had to remember that hospitals were no longer an option, yet instead it was safer to keep on my way and ponder how I could be of service to somebody later during a more planned rescue. I thought about Ronny now too. I knew that he was struggling with the same issue. Here I was, capable of helping someone just the day before and now today it's in my best interest to flee. Wishing the same for myself, I just wanted Ronny to be safe and get to Deanna and the kids because his family needed him the most right now. I felt my family, Graham included, needed me too.

As I continued on, I saw several attacks before I made it on to the Lehigh College campus area where Graham and his other graduate school friends rent a house nearby. The campus was apparently on lockdown and it seemed like there wasn't a person in sight, living or otherwise. The only sign of living, breathing humans was a checkpoint that I could see from a block away where a campus security vehicle along with two squad cars from the city of Bethlehem was parked. Since I didn't have to go through the campus to get to Graham's I didn't bother to keep going straight, instead I turned right and went over a few blocks where his house was a few properties from the corner. Right away I saw his car was gone which made me nervous as I pulled alongside the curb in the front, looking toward the house for any sign of trouble at the same time. I paid special attention to the windows as I shut off the engine and grabbed my purse, first aid bag and bat. I figured if there was any commotion inside there might be a chance that I'd see something ahead of time. I looked around the immediate area for any dead ones. It appeared safe as I got out and ran straight up the porch steps to the front door. I rang the door bell and knocked quietly. The screen door was locked and made a noise. Looking around behind me for any trouble, I walked across the open porch to get a peek into the living room window but the blinds were closed shut. Anxiety began to build in me as I fiddled around with my ring of keys to find the one that would open the door. I couldn't help but wonder where Graham might've gone or why he would leave. Perhaps his roommate Darin's condition turned for the worse and they were forced to leave. I didn't want to think about the possibility that we may have unknowingly crossed paths and he might be at my place now. I kept turning around every few seconds to make sure no one was behind me because it seemed as if one of the dead ones would stagger into the lawn at any second and I'd be too consumed with worry to even notice. Though not as successful if it were a timed test, the right key fell into place but there presented another problem; I only had a key to the oak door– not the screen door which was never locked but for good reason was locked now. The locking mechanism was solid on that door and by the looks of it I'd have a lot more trouble trying to pry it open without a crowbar or a decent flathead screwdriver. Fearing I was going to be seen by someone any minute now, I decided to head to the back door where I was sure my key would work right away. I was sure that screen had no lock on it and anything was better than just hanging around making noise at this door, waiting for something to happen to me. Before I could get around the corner of the building I was pretty sure I heard him coming and froze still just so I could listen and be sure.

Graham's car is rather sweet looking metallic, midnight blue sixty–nine Chevy Chevelle SS that once belonged to his father who kept it in pristine condition for years after he restored it. Graham received it as his college graduation present under the condition that he continued to take absolute care of it. Until now, I was never fond of the noise the aftermarket dual exhausts made when he revved the engine because that along with the white stripe down the middle– the thing screamed 'race me!' every time he turned the engine on. Because of my job working in the trauma services field I was never completely comfortable riding in it either. It was all muscle and no airbags. Graham was always responsible in most of the things he did however the friend influence was always a reason to worry. Because of the upgraded three–ninety–six engine his father added I was sometimes able to hear him coming from down the block. That was the same noise I heard now.

I leaned outward toward the street in time to see Graham turn the corner in a racing style. The car fishtailed slightly and roared a final time as he accelerated a little before coming to a stop in front of the house. He pulled up right behind my Escape and quickly shut off the engine before I could make it to the curb. I dropped everything and ran for him. By the time I made it to him he was already out and I saw that he had his shotgun in hand.

"Graham, thank God!" was all I could utter as I ignored the weapon and wrapped my arms around his neck. We kissed and embraced each other for a brief moment. He was always warm which made my heart flutter and I could feel part of the metal gun barrel somewhat pressed against my back. Honestly, they both made me feel safer now. His five inch height difference was almost no match for the energy behind my holding him. He gave me another quick kiss before cautiously looking around for any dead ones, just as I had earlier.

"I just came from your place, I left a little while after the phones went dead." He said as he bent down to help me to pick up my bag while keeping one arm around my waist still. I wanted to be upset at him for leaving the safety of his place, especially when I said I was heading to him. It didn't matter now.

"How's Darin?" I asked.

"Not good. We need to get inside." He handed me my items and pulled his keys out. We went around to the back door of the house, using caution before turning the corners.

After Graham opened the door, he cautiously looked around the immediate space before stepping inside. Once inside, I closed the door behind us. I laid down all of my belongings except for the bat and waited for a cue from Graham as to whether or not the house was still safe.

"April, I'm back now. Seanna is here too. . . April?" He called out. "I think you've met her before," He said to me.

There were just a few light footsteps we could hear approaching us in the silence. I couldn't remember April's relationship to any of the people that lived here but recall meeting her once about a year ago. All I knew was that she was a sophomore at Muhlenberg college and a little on the flaky side due to some of the things she said. At the time, her deep devotion to some of the reality programs had me worried for the younger ones in my generation.

I looked on with Graham nervously, after no one appeared in the kitchen, as he released the safety and raised the barrel of the rifle. I didn't know whether to look at him or to look at the potential threat heading our way from around the corner wall. It took about three more sounds of footsteps before ditzy little April who apparently had a death wish would appear from around the corner.

"Jesus, April! What the hell is wrong with you? Why didn't you say something— I almost shot you!" Graham exhaled as he put the safety back on and lowered the rifle. I ran over to her after looking for any obvious injuries because she wasn't the least bit startled, her face was completely red in contrast to her bright-blond, straight hair. Selfishly, I also remembered now how I wished I could get my hair to highlight as well as hers. My hair was typical of my mixed heritage where most days my golden brown tresses weren't too much to deal with but along with my in-between skin tone I dared not ever to go with just any ole blonde highlights.

"April, how's Darin?" I asked.

"He's almost dead," she said in a nasally, whiney tone. She burst into tears. Graham put his hand on her shoulder and looked at me as I shrugged my shoulders. It was all non-verbal as I could tell he wanted to know if anything could be done to help.

"Right after you left he was mumbling some weird stuff and then after a while he started twitching and shaking uncontrollably. The frickin' dummy Chad left to see about his girlfriend a few minutes ago. He said he'd come right back. I told him he shouldn't leave like you said but he left anyway." April continued, almost sobbing now.

"Sounds like a seizure, especially if he has a high grade fever," I said to them.

I walked back to my first aid bag knowing there wasn't a single thing inside of it that would help Darin. I wiggled my fingers into a fresh pair of latex gloves again and went up the stairs with Graham right behind me and April still crying, a few steps behind him. I was walking down the hall past a bathroom when I had to roll my eyes as she pointed out which room was Darin's— as if I hadn't been here before. His door was already opened slightly and the room was much cooler than the rest of the house. There was a fan on which I turned off as I reached into my bag and got the stethoscope out so I could check his heart rate and breathing. April went back into the bathroom area where I could hear her running water and she returned to apply a cold compress to his forehead and then to the scratches that were obviously infected and bruising much of his forearms and face. Darin's eyes had dark circles and a yellowish mucous was beginning to accumulate around his wounds.

I looked at Graham who knew his roommate was in trouble. Darin was unresponsive as I kept calling his name and took his pulse. You could see the sweat pooling as his t-shirt was now sticking to most of his body and his hair was drenched. His pulse was below forty beats which I thought was extremely odd, considering his temperature and sweating. If he was going to reanimate after death— which I'm sure he would, this had to be a key phase. I was about to witness in real life the stages leading up to becoming a dead one.

"For our safety, I think we should restrain him," I suggested firmly.

"But what if he wakes up? I mean he's not one of them yet. No one is sure what really happens. He's still my brother and he's not going to turn into one of those *things* wandering outside," April started in on Darin's defense.

I stared at her. Was she that naive?

"April I think she's right. It's for our safety— he's my friend." Graham calmly stated. I could see the angst in his face as he looked over his critically ill friend.

"Don't worry, I think he *is* going to wake up," I said sarcastically while I pulled the latex gloves off from my wrists first, balled them up and threw them in the trash can as I walked out of the bedroom. My intentions were to find some utility rope to restrain Darin to the bed and his little sister next to him, if necessary. I decided I was going to die of something else besides being attacked and eaten alive when I knew better what to do. I also felt like a little bit of a fool now because I didn't know where the hell in this house any rope was kept. I'd rather search for it than to stand there arguing with little

Miss Wanna-be-Dead.

Graham followed right after me, diverting my anger.

"I think I left the rope either in the basement or outside. Let's try downstairs first," he said.

Thankfully Graham kept some of his camping gear downstairs instead of in the garage because it made for much easier retrieval. I was quiet during this time because I was busy thinking about at least ten things all at once. While in the basement, he looked in one Rubbermaid bin while I looked in another. There was nothing but the noise of items being rustled around for a short while until he spoke up.

"I didn't want you to go outside, but I'm glad you made it here safely."

"Thanks for the effort to pick me up. After the phones went out I just couldn't stand and wait around there. It was horrible seeing people get attacked and torn up like that. I just can't believe it." I said to him.

"I know. Earlier this morning I knew something was up when I went in to set up the lab and check on some of the projects. Shortly after I got there, was when everyone started talking about different attacks nearby. People were getting texts and checking emails almost right away. At first everyone thought it was some huge joke but as soon as the campus police went building by building– telling everyone to go home and then all of a sudden, telling everyone to stay put. As they began locking the doors, panic started. They decided to close the campus after the emergency broadcast. I guess some students here went missing because a bunch of them were at Center City last night after the game. When people tried to leave campus this morning it'd already made it here. That's when Darin got attacked."

"It was that fast?" I couldn't imagine something like that happening to so many people, so quickly.

"We all decided to come back here when Darin started getting worse. We were able to sneak by the police, since they were obviously overwhelmed. He's been like that since right before you called. I told Chad not to leave after April showed up because I knew I had to go get you and she would be here with Darin alone. She hasn't said anything about her roommates but I guess we know what that means."

Graham looked under a folded tarp where he found some rope.

"I was hoping for utility rope because it's thicker and a little more durable, but this should do it," he said.

I didn't know my strings but I considered Graham to be at the top of his rope game. He was frequently outdoors and used various equipment that needed rope to help with research and other projects that they were working on for their thesis. Without a doubt I would follow Graham's instruction because I loved and trusted him. I always admired the way he analyzed things differently than I did, which was always complementary over being offensive. I looked on as he firmly held the rope, pulling on it and testing it to be sure it could handle the repetitive stress. I wasn't sure if Darin would ever consciously know he was being tied down but either way I'm sure he wouldn't like it.

"What are we going to do with him, if he changes?" I asked quietly.

"We'll do what we have to do. Until then, he's still—…"

"I know he's still our friend. I just need to know that you can let go if and when the time comes." I figured Graham might be reluctant to write his friend off so quickly, especially since they've known each other since high school. I didn't want to offend him but I could tell we were on the same page and to know that was enough for me. As I looked around the basement for other things useful, Graham placed the rope on a table, walked over to me and put his arms around me. I don't know if it was for his sake or mine but I was willing to be strong for him so I held him in return. His warmth made it easy for me to feel safe again and I could smell remnants of the *Declaration* eau de toilette spray I bought for him back at the start of his studies in January. I knew it was an odd gift selection but I always went with my gut feelings and spontaneity. I guessed he would like the scent and thankfully, I was right. I could've stood there in silence with him for eternity because aside from the whole reason we were in the basement, everything seemed completely normal and safe. We could not see the world around us falling apart into chaos from where we stood and it certainly didn't appear as if just two floors above us, someone we both knew and loved was dying.

"You know I'm with you until the end, right?" Graham spoke in soft tones to me.

"I know, me too. I love you." I said in return, looking into his brownish-green eyes, hoping again to wakeup from this nightmare scenario. My fearfully fluttering heart told me this was instead, nothing I'd wake up from.

I closed my eyes and squeezed him one last time before we separated. I knew that from this point on if he had it his way, Graham would never be far from me and I certainly hoped there would be a million more embraces and intimate moments before we met our end. Feeling it might be of use eventually, I picked up a flashlight from one of the tables and he grabbed the rope before we both heard April cry out from the upstairs bedroom. We both glanced at each other and Graham darted up the stairs in a quick motion. I was a few steps behind him when I heard April yell for us again.

"Graham, you guys get up here *quick*!" She yelled with even more intensity.

Graham rounded the hallway and was up the second set of stairs when I heard April yell out again that Darin was not breathing anymore— this time she was at top of the stairs and a little more frantic. In my mind, I wasn't sure how I would go about trying to resuscitate him because the only thing I knew for sure was that whatever Darin and countless others had— it was extremely contagious. I got to the room just in time to see both of them hovering over Darin's lifeless body and Graham starting to do CPR. He began doing the chest compressions and soon as he went over to breathe air into Darin's mouth, I abruptly stopped him.

"Wait! I'm not sure you should do that," I warned. This of course made April irate.

"Why aren't you helping him? You're a fucking paramedic— you're supposed to save his life!" She ranted on more and screamed various obscenities at me.

I looked at her, wanting so badly to engage her stupidity. From memory I was able to recall her lack of fondness for me. This was the perfect opportunity to lash out.

"He's gone, okay? Look at him April! What do you think is gonna happen to Graham when he swaps spit with him by breathing air into his mouth?"

I didn't mean to make it sound like a romantic affair but I needed blondie here to get the point. I picked up the rope that Graham dropped and grabbed a pair of scissors from off of the desk that was nearby a window. I glanced outside where I saw not one– but two people, dead, walking aimlessly around a few houses down from us toward the middle of the block. As soon as April saw what I was doing she continued on with her rant.

"What are you *doing*?" she yelled.

"I'm tying him to the bed." I replied simply, measuring out enough rope for each limb. Graham glanced over at the now deceased Darin and took the first section of rope I cut.

"Oh no, you're not! You just helped him die and now you're going to tie my dead brother up like he's some kind of animal?"

"We don't have time to discuss this," I said while continuing to cut the rope, not even giving her eye contact. I had about three or four pieces cut. Graham walked over to take them from me so he could start tying each limb to the headboard and each limb to the frame from the foot of the bed since there was no footboard on the full sized bed. He asked me to cut some longer pieces and a few extra to use, just to be safe.

She was just about to say something when her voice became distorted from changing its pitch too quickly. From the corner of my eye, I saw Graham jump back which made me automatically move as well. April wailed in pain as I looked just in time to see Darin's hand grab her arm and his head burrow right into the area between her neck and shoulder, ripping flesh from her like something out of a wildlife show. Darin pushed his sister onto the floor and took another bite out of her shoulder while she cried out in terrible pain. For the second time in two hours I saw shock remove a person from their ability to fight back. Graham grabbed Darin's other arm and tried to pull him off of her. It then only made him become a target as Darin now refocused his attention towards him. I dropped everything and tried to help, stepping over April who was now on her back side holding her arm, wailing in an ear piercing tone. Graham was struggling with Darin now trying to stop his attack. They knocked over a book stand and a lamp in their scuffles, causing the cord that was still plugged in to trip Graham. They both ended up on the floor– Graham on the bottom near April as she bled profusely while trying to move out of the way herself. I did what I thought was best and tried to pull Darin off of Graham with all my strength. From what I found, it would be no easy task. Darin was now groaning and gnashing his bloodied teeth but again turned his attentions this time to me. From the second I grabbed at him, I inadvertently helped him back onto his feet. I was nearest to the bed and was forced back on it in an effort to distance myself from Darin who had now lunged at me trying for more chunks of flesh. I saw his eyes up close and I could tell that he was no longer Darin. Some kind of wildness had replaced the serenity and calm that everyone, me included, saw in them every day until now. There was redness around his former dark brown irises followed by a gray-yellow haze that used to be white. For what seemed like an eternity I was able to see what I missed the last time up close with the dead one in my apartment building with Ronny.

"Darin . . . . Darin . . . *please*, stop!" I struggled to scream out while trying to push him away. He paid no attention and recognized nothing.

I was obviously the weaker one and I could see behind him, Graham scrambling to stand up and grab the shotgun that he sat by the doorway earlier. I fought tirelessly to keep him off of me, to avoid any bites and scratches and struggled to position my right foot up against Darin's body. This was not easy as he had an extra firm grip on my arms and the sleeves of my zip-up jacket. I saw Graham with the shotgun aimed and he yelled something that I couldn't hear because I was too worried about my own life. I was nearly out of energy when I gave one last burst of power to my leg and kicked outward which surprisingly forced Darin off of me into the wall by the desk. He quickly regrouped to come back at me but not before I heard the exploding sound of the shotgun followed by the discharge of the empty shell and a second shot to follow. The first shot hit Darin in the abdomen in which the force pushed him again into the wall causing tiny clusters of blood to splatter behind him. He reacted only to regain his footing until the second shot pierced his face and went on further through his head putting even more blood on the walls. Darin's face was now almost unrecognizable as he dropped to the floor, permanently stopped from all functioning.

Graham set the gun down and came over to both of us as April was still on the floor shivering in pain and crying from the events that just took place. I'm sure it was traumatic for her to see her brother's body and face taken apart like that- it was traumatic for all of us, however I felt sorry for her now. I bent over her to examine the damage done and saw all of the blood on the floor underneath her. Disregarding the pathogenic harm from not using gloves I attempted to reach out to her in order to sit her up but she wasn't going for it.

"Don't *you* touch me!" She said wincing from the pain.

Her back was almost completely wet from blood. I ignored her and helped her to sit on the bed.

"I think we should get out of this room," Graham added, surveying the area.

"Let's go downstairs so I can dress these wounds," I tried to comfort the girl who hated me, as best as I could. She jerked away from me once again.

"Why should I let *you* help me? So you can help me just like you helped my brother?" She stood up now looking at me with more contempt in her eyes.

"April calm down please, let her help you." Graham suggested as April now turned appearing to lash out at him next.

"All you're going to do is wait around so you can figure out when you can tie me up and kill me next. My brother trusted you Graham. You were his best friend!" She yelled.

"It's not like that and *yes* I was his best friend, he was mine."

"Whatever . . . is the next bullet in that shotgun mine? You gonna put me down too Graham?" April said then started sobbing. Graham took a deep breath but didn't respond because he knew she was testing his tolerance. She slowly walked out of the room and Graham and I followed before taking one last look at Darin who was now slumped awkwardly in the corner. I didn't know what was on her mind but I knew that she'd have at least a few hours if she was not seriously incapacitated– which she seemingly wasn't. I could tell that she always had a thing for Graham all the years she's known him so it was obvious to me that he would be the one to convince her to do anything. After all, my efforts to be decent to her had failed.

With the adrenaline wearing off and my breathing returning to a somewhat normal range, I took the blanket off of the bed and hung it over Darin's slumped body. I was too consumed with fear to handle his body any more than that for now. If we were lucky the time would come to deal with his remains, to perhaps to recall more pleasant memories and say goodbye to someone who I felt had three times his age in years left to live than what was just dealt to him since this morning. I closed the door quietly as I said a prayer for his soul.

Once the three of us were back on the first floor Graham started to reason with April. I decided to hang back and let him take the lead. My part simply would be to not aggravate her, to be silent, and attempt to take care of her the best way that I could. I had minimal supplies that I would make do with and at least try to cleanse and dress the wounds– even though it made little sense to do so. After all, what else could she get now– an infection? She already had one as far as that was concerned and even I'd be overjoyed if all she walked away with from this was a staph infection instead.

"April, I know after what just happened that you now understand why we're being cautious," Graham stated bluntly. He continued on.

"I know Darin, he is– was my buddy, you know that. I also know that he would not have wanted to be one of those things. It's because of those *things* that he ended up dying and nothing else. What I shot was not your brother."

I stood there listening in support because I believed everything Graham said now was true. It was almost too much to deal with. I tried my best to not think about Darin's life as I knew it because it wouldn't help anyone right now, especially April, if I said anything. I felt as if I shot Darin, regardless of the fact that he no longer had a pulse, breath or was his self. I didn't want to just start working on April's bloody wounds without her permission so I took her contemplative silence as a sign that maybe she understood Graham's point and was thinking about the scenario in a different perspective now.

"May I take a look at your shoulder April?" I said in my kindest tone after minute or so.

April was going to say something but she didn't get a chance. She wasn't yelling when she started so I figured my request might've been granted. The sound of the shotgun along with all of the commotion and her high-pitched yelling must've attracted a few visitors- the ones I saw earlier I presume because there was a scraping sound on the front door. It would've seemed like a normal knock except it was lazier, as if the fists were dragging against the screen door after they hit it. They were pretty strong knocks too. I figure if the door wasn't locked they might have succeeded in opening it from force alone. We all must've heard it at the exact same moment because we stopped everything to listen further. Graham and I both cautiously walked to where we could see the front door. From where I stood I could see our suspicions verified as the door vibrated from the outside force.

Graham whispered quietly for me to stay put as he crept slowly toward the front windows, to take a look. The house had new flooring so they hardly made a sound as he walked, luckily. The blinds in the living room window were still closed shut so he opened one ever so slightly, and after a few seconds let it back down, slowly. Walking both quickly and carefully I waited for him to get close enough to ask how many there were because it was obvious by the look on his face exactly who it was already.

"There are three of them." He whispered to me, loud enough however for April to hear.

"The loud noise must've drawn them in, what should we do?" I asked.

"If we stay quiet, maybe they'll leave." Graham responded.

"Why don't you just shoot them like you shot Darin!" April said in a loud, sarcastic tone.

My patience was running short with her now. If I weren't a decent person I could see myself actually dragging her outside for them to feed on but of course that would only solve one minor problem. It would probably just make things worse by attracting more of them because I'm thinking even then she wouldn't shut up until they ate the last of her vocal cords. April was red with anger and I knew she would do nothing to help us now- especially with her fate already sealed. I would not even address her outrage but Graham looked at her with disgust. He chose to engage her this time and I felt it was good enough to be from both of us.

"April, all these years I have known you- you have never been anything but childish and self absorbed. You'll never understand why we do anything because our actions since this morning are beyond you and your scope of thinking. I'm not even sure you'll understand by the time you die today. You feel everyone else should just lie down and die with you since you lost the chance to save your life when it was arguably worth saving. Personally, that's just only one reason why you and I never had a thing in common. The greatest thing you can do besides earning your way into hell is to just keep your mouth closed now."

Graham said all of this to her without raising his voice beyond a low tone. By the time he finished I felt bad for her, aside from all the negative things she's said to me today. The sad truth was she's a young girl dying right in front of us and although the mechanism behind her exact cause of death was not in plain sight for me to see, I imagined the virus causing the skin around her bite to bruise and she was probably already developing a fever. Symptomatically, I now saw her as someone who needed to be treated and she deserved the same dignity as everyone else on their last day. Graham's words must've struck a nerve in her because her eye's and cheeks turned red and tears began to fall. She was absolutely silent now and I could see the grief and pain consume her. In such a few words Graham told her exactly why after all of these years he'd never pursued his best friend's sister and though I was far from defending her, I could sympathize with her heartbreak.

I wasn't sure now what to say or do, except for the repeated attempts by the dead to get through the front door; all of this deserved a moment of contemplation. The screen door shook and rattled as they mustered on in their efforts. Who knows for how long they would be there before the door frame finally gave way or they got smart and simply broke through one of the many windows the house had. Graham ran his fingers across his forehead in critical thought before he vocally contemplated our options.

"I think it'll help if we create a distraction. If I can get outside and down the street I could divert them in another direction." Graham said.

"You can't go outside to them! You'd be handing yourself right over. You don't know how many others might be nearby!" I argued. The three he saw could be only the beginning.

Graham walked down the hallway toward the side of the house closest to the middle of the block. I followed behind him out of curiosity. The window he looked out of was a partially stained glass window that had beautiful blue and green edging around the center of a smaller square of clear regular glass. Through it he was able to look at the house next door and then up toward its roof.

"I should be able to get over without being on the ground level or going outside. Chad's room is closer to the next house and I think I could get on to their roof from his window. I only need to be loud enough to draw them away."

"I don't know," was all I could answer as I shook my head.

He was talking about jumping onto a roof whereas I was hoping for something that required a little less skill and didn't include a 25 foot drop. I started to suggest something but got immediately distracted as there was now a noise coming from the back door. Graham and I both quietly rushed toward the source of the commotion. Before he could tell April to step away from the kitchen it was clear that she was the one responsible for it. The back door was left wide open because April took off. Neither of us could see which direction she went aside from going through the back yard where the gate was also left open. Graham stepped on to the back porch and looked in both directions.

"I can't tell which way she ran," he said as he exhaled in frustration.

"Maybe she thinks she'll do better out there than in here, I don't know if I blame her."

"I can't say which is better but I know I wouldn't want to become one of those things," he replied.

Graham stood outside for a few seconds longer then stepped back inside. Reluctantly he closed the door, locked it and double checked its durability by jiggling the knob. He looked out of the window for any sign of April for a moment before giving up and going to retrieve another box of bullets for his shotgun. I turned my own attentions to the front door, taking a moment to see if I could hear any of the same noises we heard earlier with the dead ones trying to get in through the front door. Fortunately, I heard nothing so I took my chances– walking slowly down the short hallway and across the living room. I paid close attention to the windows for any shadows to indicate whether or not they were still lingering on the porch. Once I got close enough, I leaned forward to peek through and to my surprise, I saw no one. I quickly checked in both directions and said barely above a whisper, "I think they've left," to Graham who was now in the other hallway with his own backpack out. To my misfortune I was wrong because one the dead ones must've been further off to the side from the view I had through the space of the tiny blind. One of them must have saw the blind move aside from my cautious efforts because without more than a second worth of effort– the window next to mine suddenly shook and broke under the outside force. It gave me little time to react as the dead man fell inward and on to the living room floor. I screamed as loud as my vocal cords would allow as I saw Graham dart back into the kitchen. I was hoping he'd return with the shotgun that hadn't let us down yet. There must've been at least two more dead ones whose hands and arms I could see now attempting to follow the first dead man who was now in Graham's living room and coming after me.

Where the hell was my bat I needed it?

I managed to grab the first object I felt might do some damage, which at the moment was going to have to be an empty vase that sat on a bookshelf within arm's reach. In that same moment the dead man that had fallen in was now back on his feet and right at my face. I grabbed the vase and swung it around as quickly and with as much force as I could, connecting with the side of his pale, bruised face. The vase shattered, however the man only stumbled sideways a few feet, failing to feel pain. What might've cost me my life was that as he stumbled back, he grabbed my left arm which pulled me forward with him into the line of fire. I knew this because I heard several loud blasts and unwillingly fell to the floor with the dead man's fingers still clenching on to my jacket and sleeves.

I heard Graham yell my name as my left shoulder now stung beyond belief. I fell onto the floor feeling the warm moisture that could only have come from my own blood flowing outward. To make matters worse, the dead man was not permanently down yet either because he continued his task apparently unbothered. For the third and final time, I presumed, I would now both see and experience personally the same shock and pain that prevented the others, including April, from moving to save their own lives. I wormed and squealed hoping something would happen to prevent me from being attacked but I knew both the opportunity for help and my life, were running short. I used my unwounded and free arm to try and stop the man but I knew with the blood loss my decreasing strength would be no match.

Where the hell was Graham?

Adding to my pain and suffering, the dead man– who smelled of the same familiar clay and rotted meat odor as the man from my apartment, crawled over to me and with his body partially covering mine, he took a bite out of my left forearm as I struggled to block him from attacking more vital areas like my neck or ripping my organs out like I witnessed earlier. I screamed again in absolute horror. His teeth were normal but I've never been bitten by another person, let alone the mouth of a dead person. Nevertheless, it hurt all the same. It might as well have been a dog or a shark because he now had at least a few inches of the flesh of my forearm in his mouth. The attack came to an abrupt end as he too was forced to stop suddenly when another loud blast and a bullet ripped into the upper portion of the dead man's head causing him to collapse– the upper part of his body falling on mine. While trying to diffuse the pain in my shoulder and the blood that was now freely flowing from both wounds, I let out a loud gasp and looked to my left side in time to see a large black boot worn by a man uniformed in black gear that was similar to what someone wore on the *SWAT* team. His face was partially covered but I could see he had blue, squinty eyes– or at least, they were squinting at me. He held onto a long, semi-automatic weapon which he lowered just as with one arm he pulled the dead man off of me and knelt down to survey what happened.

"The doc's not gonna like this," he said in a simplistic tone.

"Is it her?" Another unfamiliar voice from the kitchen asked.

"Yeah, we got her. Radio the base, tell them we're done here and will be back en route with an ETA of about an hour and a half," the blue-eyed, simplistic voice replied, his eyes never left mine.

I also heard someone mention something about the loss of blood and getting me loaded up, which I didn't know exactly what they were referring to. Where the hell could I be going in this mess? No one identified themselves as being police officers or anything else. I knew most of the medics and officers in the area by name or face, yet I couldn't tell who he was. I heard Graham's voice behind me– possibly outside in the backyard now and he was not happy or being peaceful about our rescue, if this was one. His unsuccessful attempt to find out just who our unknown rescuers were was, of course, also on my mind but was not my top concern as I lay on the floor bleeding out and trying to maintain consciousness.

I tried to move as I heard Graham get escorted out further away. I heard several more gunshots come from the front porch before a voice mentioned the urgency of returning back to base before this location becomes another 'hot zone'. Just as I tried to roll over to get up, a hand landed on my chest– pushing me downward.

"Lay still, Seanna." the blue-eyed man spoke again.

I felt his hand also hold the top of my head perhaps in an attempt to comfort me. There was overwhelming discomfort however, so I unsuccessfully tried to move my head again. Of course there was nothing more I could do.

"Which one of you shot me?" I asked after several sighs and moans. I was losing my strength against the overwhelming pain and stinging sensation.

"Are you sure it wasn't your boyfriend?" Blue eyes responded.

"I know it wasn't him, this is a single bullet- I think," I answered him slowly- taking deep breaths. I closed my eyes.

"Smart girl. Someone here owes Miss Burges an apology," he said as he spoke up for the others to hear.

A few seconds later, the blue-eyed man stepped back and I felt myself being moved, involuntarily onto what had to be a portable stretcher from how the thick canvas mesh felt against my back. I grunted in pain as two pairs of gloved hands applied pressure and gauze to both of the wounds in an attempt to stop the bleeding. I couldn't help but to close my eyes as I felt myself being carried through the back way into the kitchen and out of the back door, down the porch stairs. Several more shots were fired from outside as I could hear a flurry of movement around me. The two people who carried me, a man and a woman were not armed as they whisked me through Graham's backyard. From my view, there were four or five armored vehicles. The one in the middle was converted from a passenger van which I was being loaded into. The other vehicles were identical and were a cross between a *Hummer* and one of those *Brinks* trucks and looked as if they meant business. I heard the ETA of ninety minutes being repeated into a radio in the background and Graham's voice once again, which this time erupted a little more of a reaction out of me.

"Wouldn't make more sense for me to ride with her?" Graham questioned.

"Mr. Randall, please, you're both going to the same place. She needs care right now. This way to the other vehicle," another voice said.

"She needs me too," Graham argued to no avail.

The argument was cut off by a question from the blue-eyed man, asking about the confirmed dead man upstairs. Graham verified that it was one of the residents of the house and his friend by name. Before I could hear any more of the conversation, the doors of the vehicle I was in were closed and I was secured to my stretcher with straps which came from a bed underneath that must've been converted from a row of seats from the side. I fought hard to stay awake as the two who carried me in now took vital signs and addressed my shoulder and my forearm in the exact same manner that I would as if it were myself on duty instead. The back door of the vehicle opened once again as we were joined by the blue-eyed man. He closed the door and told the driver to let the others know that we could move now and within seconds I felt the vehicle spur into gear from its idle. The sound of the diesel engine was not unfamiliar as it shifted and we moved forward. I began to get anxious as the blue-eyed man took off his helmet and skull cap that hid much of his identity. In addition to his blue eyes, he had sandy blonde hair that was graying ever so slightly at the sides. I blinked a few times to stay focused in an effort to try and remember every little detail—the creases at the sides of his mouth, the shape of his nose, any little thing because I knew I was not worthy of the attention for this kind of rescue operation. Maybe the mayor deserved it, perhaps a councilman even, but not me, Seanna Burges of Allentown, Pennsylvania.

"Eighty-six over sixty-two with a GSW to the left scapula and bite to her left mid forearm." the man checking my vitals said.

"Start her on the antibiotic with the morphine," blue eyes said.

I couldn't help the physiological response I had because I was out of it. The last words I heard were, "Hurry up, I think she's going into shock," which was not said with the right amount of urgency, I think. I figured I was pretty much screwed from the moment I was shot and the dead man sunk his teeth into my arm. Now I wouldn't have a clue as to where I was going or the ability to even ask. I slipped further down into darkness as the blue-eyed man leaned down and simply said, "Take it easy, Seanna."

Chapter Four

The sun was bright and the temperatures were nearing one hundred on this day in late July. The year was 1996 and my mother, Ivy insisted on throwing my seventh birthday party that day. I always wondered why she was so enthusiastic about birthday parties until she told me that as a child she always had to celebrate her birthdays with her sister Sandra. She explained to me that ever since she was a little girl she hoped that when she was older and had girls of her own they would always have parties individually so they could each be unique and have a choice with the theme they wanted. I only had a handful of close friends in grade school so my mother invited the neighbors and their children along. She had gone overboard with the decorations this year. She always went with pink and yellow and little bit of purple in some variation with my parties and today was no different. I sat in the living room of our home in suburban Philadelphia, waiting for the guests to arrive. Wearing my jean skirt, yellow short-sleeve top and yellow sandals I was hoping for only a small turnout-there was something about the heat that day that caused me to be uncooperative. I insisted that I did my own hair that day and opted to do two long ponytails because I saved my allowance of five dollars and used it to buy some multi-colored hair clips and barrettes at the store. With my lop-sided ponytails, I sat for what seemed like forever waiting on the guests to show up and finally, they did. With the bright sun and heat, one by one, people trailed in as my mother glided from the kitchen, making last minute food preparations, into the living room and front entry way every time the doorbell rang. She was always excited to see people and remembered details of their lives for conversation. I would just smile and stare and watch their interactions.

My father Jackson, Sr. was mostly a quiet, content and happy man but today on my birthday he seemed a bit distracted. I saw a few times where my mother would talk to him and it took him a longer time to respond. In my opinion, it wasn't because he didn't know how to answer, he was very smart and attentive- it just seemed as if he wasn't listening. I even teased him by asking once, "Daddy, how old am I?" and it took him a long while to answer. Only after I pressed him he answered quickly and got up to use the phone in his office space or the den as we called it when he was not using it for his engineering-related work. I remember shifting my focus away from my mother and her greetings to our visitors and looking into his office as he talked on the phone in what seemed like an intense debate with the another person. I wasn't used to him talking in such a tone so of course this had my full attention until he saw me and closed the door. Once the guests were numerous enough he came out of the office but I knew that something was bothering him because of the way he acted for the rest of the night. My mother's mood that day never wavered as she was always capable of entertaining her guests.

It was the sound of my mother's cheerful voice that woke me up. Sadly though, she wasn't anywhere around. I opened my eyes to find that I was lying in a hospital bed, in a gown, hooked up to several monitors and both of my arms were restrained. It seemed like I was not in an actual hospital because the large room was sparsely decorated, was missing windows and things like medical supply cabinets. It generally felt like something other than a health care center. Other than the bed and the machines, there were only plain white walls, one side table and lighting that was too dim and stylish for any hospital ward. There was also a single professional looking office chair next to my bed. I felt quite groggy and would've thought that the events that I remembered where just a dream if it weren't for the dull pain in my forearm and shoulder. I had an IV in my right arm which was connected to a drug delivery pump and an oxygen sensor on my finger that I was all too familiar with from my line of work. It was hard for me to look up to see which medications I'd been given. I would easily be able to figure out the more commonly used ones from the label on the IV bags. The pain in my shoulder combined with the limb restraints restricted even the slightest movement in my neck so I spent a few minutes looking at the ceiling, searching the sectioned surface above to recall recent events. Looking down, I saw that my left forearm was bandaged. Remembering why it was caused me to panic.

I tried to pull on the restraints but I knew they were designed to handle that, so I gave up. I heard the machines behind me react to the increase of my blood pressure and pulse and I knew that somewhere, somebody saw this same reaction on their monitors too. I knew that typically someone should be assigned to watch the monitors but since this probably wasn't a hospital there was no telling what kind of system they'd be running. I worried about Graham and felt even more uneasy because I didn't know what happened to him after we left his house. From the back of the armored van I couldn't tell which direction they drove in or if Graham was even allowed to go to the same place I'm in now. I hoped that I was just being irrational and perhaps I really was in the room of a real hospital and that I would find out everything is now under control. Maybe all of what I thought happened never did and I instead have managed to develop some psychosis and this is actually some mental facility. I'd be overjoyed if that was the case— I think. Still not feeling at ease and also slightly lightheaded, I rested my head back on the single pillow. Thinking about reality, I closed my eyes for a second to contemplate the bite on my arm and how long I'd have left before I'd end up like the many others I'd seen staggering around. How long would it take before I was like Darin, April and poor little Ruthie. I tried calculating how many hours I might have lost. Meanwhile, the door to the room suddenly opened, temporarily halting my thoughts.

A youthful-looking Middle Eastern man wearing glasses and a lab coat walked in. I squinted trying to look at his badge to get a name or see a hospital but it was too difficult in the dim light. "Miss Burges." he said in a surprisingly American accent as he approached me. When he spoke, I figured he was likely from India or Pakistan, raised here though.

"You can call me Seanna. Who are you and where am I?"

"Okay Seanna, my name is Dr. Sainiraj Chavan. I'm a research assistant here."

"Are you a medical doctor?" I interrupted him quickly.

"I am. I've also attained my Ph.D. in Bio-Genetics-..."

"Am I in a hospital?" I interrupted again. I was usually more polite when I met people but he'd have to understand that today, I wanted the short version.

"You're in a safe place where we can monitor and take care of you."

The simplicity of his nondisclosure wasn't going to suffice me- not one bit. The monitors sounded again at the increase of my vital signs. Dr. Chavan looked up at the monitor in response and warned, "I'm going to need you to remain calm Miss-Seanna." I knew I had no control over what those monitors were sounding over but I realized something was different because I actually felt it now. I felt like the virus was in me and it was like a rush of heat with chills to follow. The wounds on my arm and shoulder were starting to burn with pain.

"How long do I have, Dr. Chavan?" I wasted no time before asking another question. Ignoring all the pain I was in, I sat straight up in the bed. "Where *am* I?" I said in a louder tone.

"You're at a research facility in New Jersey," he said in a low voice.

"What's going on with me? I'm infected, right? That's why I'm restrained? Am I going to end up like the others?" I had so much running through my mind I could barely keep up with it. He must've sensed my anxiety and took pity on me because he hesitated, looked at the door, as if someone else might come into the room and catch him divulging secrets. He sat down in the chair next to my bed, leaned forward and looked into my eyes. I looked at him right back waiting for anything he could tell me.

"I'll tell you this because I know you are afraid and have many questions," he began but I saw that he glanced at the door once more.

I was all ears. "Yes." I said as I rested back on the pillow, easily exhausted from just sitting upward.

"You're being studied. You do have the virus. You were bitten, you remember?"

"Yes, I remember." How could I forget?

"You're experiencing some of the similar symptoms from the infection but my team and I believe your prognosis could possibly be non-fatal versus all the others who have the very same thing and expire as a result." He informed me.

"Okay. So you think there's a chance I won't die from this?" Suddenly I felt really warm again and my arm radiated in so much pain I had to remain still and close my eyes. He gave me a few seconds to recover while he retrieved a pair of disposable gloves from the drawer on the nightstand and slid them on. He asked for consent which I quickly gave then examined underneath the bandage where I was also able to see the once bite-sized wound that was now sutured into a slightly crooked little line. What was missing that I'd noticed from the other scratches and bites I'd seen, was the absence of bruising and build-up of mucous that had accumulated in small amounts in and around wherever the dead ones managed to break the skin. Don't get me wrong, the injury hurt like hell still but visibly- the injury looked less like an infection was present.

"I don't have much time to explain but it seems like you are tolerating this virus much better." He sealed the bandage back to how it was, discarded his gloves and reached for the chart at the foot of the bed to write some notes down.

"Why am I feeling so hot and tired? Do I have a fever?"

"Well, you were shot and there may or may not be some tiny fragments of the bullet in your shoulder still. Another one of my colleagues removed the bullet so you'll probably have another X-ray now that you're more stable."

The doctor stood up to look the monitors and wrote additional things down on his chart. I didn't see a clock in the room, which was probably on purpose. I asked him about the time and was surprised to find out that it was still the same day but now almost midnight, at least nine hours after the incident at Graham's house. Speaking of, I asked him about Graham hoping he'd continue to be open with me but he answered curtly with "I wouldn't know. I've been assigned only to you." What kind of answer was that? I figure he should at least know how many people came into the facility along with me.

"I know that there will be someone coming in to talk to you soon, but for safety reasons, this is all that I can tell you. There is a lot about your medical history that I don't know and-..." Dr. Chavan was interrupted as the door quickly swung open and in walked a man that may have been about the same age as the doctor, only this man was shorter and instead of a lab coat he wore a blazer and jeans. The man also wore glasses and was definitely American- one could tell by the way he walked. I don't know if he was Dr. Chavan's colleague or superior but he carried himself as if he had some kind of authority.

"How are things going?" The man said as he walked up to Dr. Chavan. It was obvious he wasn't talking to me since there was no eye contact.

"I'm looking over her vitals now so I can update them with the lab. Her temp is still the same, we'll do another CBC for comparison shortly," Dr. Chavan informed him.

"Good. You can discontinue the Polymyxin after this dose is finished. We'll have the other stuff after that. I'll want a complete report from you guys in the morning. He'll want to see it too." He paused after glancing at me- which I looked directly at him as well. "I just spoke with Sinclair- He thinks the progress is good overall . Well, I'll see you in the morning then."

The man, who stood in way to block his badge so I couldn't see it, walked out of the room as quickly as he did coming in. As soon as the door closed I pressed on with the doctor because I knew he would be the only source I had for information until a better one came along.

"Who was that?" I asked.

"He's from administration."

"There's going to be a meeting about me in the morning?"

"There is a meeting in the morning; you are a part of the agenda."

"Polymyxin– that's used to treat infections."

"You're right." Again he was curt. He avoided any eye contact with me and looked only at the chart, perhaps reading previous notes as he flipped back through the few pages.

"Listen, I know you said you can't talk but I'm being treated and have a right to know what's going on from the diagnosis to treatments and pretty much everything else. It's obvious with everything that's happening that I won't be going anywhere. There's nowhere to go, you know that." I pleaded with him. I tried not to sound desperate.

Chavan looked at me from the corner of his eyes while he was still taking notes. He wrote down a few more things before he flipped the rest of the stack of papers back and sat the clipboard on the chair. I heard the monitors beep in response and instantly felt the surge of heat again along with the pain– which when from dull and numb to significant in a matter of seconds. I closed my eyes tightly in hopes that it would pass. I was afraid now because this time the pain was everywhere– my nerves seemed to shake with it as the most severe portions were still at the site of both wounds. I let out a gasp which got the doctor moving as he reached into his lab coat and pulled out a syringe. He found the port on my IV, unscrewed the cap and attached the syringe to the tube.

"This is Dilaudid." He said as he pushed the medication into the tubes that went into my veins. "It will treat your pain and help you relax. " He grabbed another syringe filled with a solution of sodium chloride to inject as standard procedure.

"Something's not right about this. Please help me Dr. Chavan." I shut my eyes again in pain because it was all I could do. I was still restrained.

He took the syringe out after it was emptied and attached the IV tube back in its original place. He patted the top of my uninjured right shoulder as I started to drift off from the effects. I could feel myself get lighter as my head disconnected from the rest of my body. Not able to consider everything, I felt like every little thing was taken away– including my concern. I no longer had the power to put up a fuss. My mouth was still active however as I pleaded with the young doctor my concerns.

"I need you to help me, Dr. Chavan," I didn't mean for it to come out like that.

"I know– we'll give our best shot." He replied as he patted my arm.

"No, you don't understand, I *need* to find Graham. I want to see him before I–.."

"It is my intent to help you, Seanna."
Did he just say what he meant, no, maybe he did care. Damn these drugs.

CHAPTER FIVE

I slowly emerged from unconsciousness and what seemed like total obscurity. I was still in the same basic room as before with the machines and monitors behind me. As if I needed more proof of the prior events, I took a moment to think in sequential order all of the people I'd come into contact with; Ronny showing up at my apartment to tell me there were deceased people running around and attacking anyone alive; my reluctance to stay in my apartment after I tried to call my parents and brother; Graham's brief conversation with me before the phones went out; Ronny and I leaving the apartment; Ruthie's infection; Darin's infection; Darin's death; the brawl which left April infected too; the dead ones busting through his living room window and finally my own little scuffle which left me shot and infected thereafter by God knows who. It was the dull pain in my shoulder that verified my reality and as a result of it I'd been taken to some facility in New Jersey according to a research doctor so I could be studied and monitored. If I remembered correctly, the doctor told me it seemed as if I might not 'expire' like everyone else who got infected.

Why was I still being restrained then?

The door to the room opened again, interrupting my thoughts. This time there was a different man accompanied by the research doctor. They both approached my bedside where the doctor held in his hand a few multi-colored test tubes for blood collection. He introduced himself to me again while the other man stood back and observed me.

"Seanna, do you remember me? I'm Dr. Chavan."

"I do. Your first name is Sainiraj." I pronounced it to the best of my ability.

"It is," he said as he glanced over at the other man who gave a quick smirk.

"Seanna, I'm going to take a few tubes of your blood for further testing. In the meanwhile, tell me how you got infected and what you're feeling," I nodded my head and the doctor grabbed another pair of gloves, disconnected the IV port and began the process of drawing blood into three test tubes. I replied to his request and looked down in time to see him pull a forth tube out of the pocket from his lab coat. I focused on the different colors on the caps of the tubes he was filling as I tried to describe in my best words what was basically any person's worst nightmare.

"I guess I don't know how I feel right now– I've never felt like this... My arm and shoulder still hurt but the pains all over aren't as bad as before," I glanced down at my arm and back at the doctor as he quickly removed one tube and then added another to fill in its place. Before I knew it, I switched topics.

"Why am I still in these restraints? You told me I'm not turning into one them yet. I promise I'll let you know if I feel weird or something. I've seen it before when it happened to others– they die first before coming back."

"I know it's awkward, Seanna. Please be patient with us," he replied as he switched to yet another tube for collection. I looked past him and saw that the other man was still observing all of my actions. What was he there for? Once our eyes met I gave him a quick scowl before shifting my focus back to Dr. Chavan and his blood draw. I sighed in frustration before another wave of pain swarmed in on me. I did my best to not react to it because I knew it would go against everything I said only seconds ago. Even worse, I didn't need two people to witness this contradiction– it wouldn't help my efforts to lose the restraints one bit. Detecting the change in my vitals, the alarm on the monitors sounded, giving away any last chance of keeping the horrible pain a secret any longer. I gripped the railings on the bed but there was nothing that would distract or deter this pain attack from running its course.

"Oh my God... this hurts!" was all I could muffle through clenched teeth as I squeezed my eyes shut.

"Where does it hurt Seanna?" The doctor questioned.

"Everywhere!"

"Lie back. I'll get you something for it," he tried to assure me.

"No, I don't want to lose any more time."

Aside from my fidgeting, the doctor was able to finish collecting the last two tubes of blood which I opened my eyes in time to see him slip the last one back into his lab coat pocket. Dr. Chavan was standing with his back to the other man in such a way it was doubtful that while observing my behavior he would actually see the test tube going into his lab coat pocket. Dr. Chavan finished the draw, handed the three tubes to the man who by now held a plastic collection bag and told him he was going to stay with me until the pain subsided. The man gladly accepted the vials and rushed out of the room. Dr. Chavan quickly stepped over to an intercom that was behind my bed on the wall. I heard him call for someone to bring another dose of the pain medication and antiviral. I was shivering from the pain by the time he finished the order.

"Are you sure I'm not dying?" I said as I took in deep breaths from the drain of energy.

"The truth is, anyone else bit at the same time as you would've likely expired by now. From all the scientific facts and evidence we have, every minute you've been alive since about two hours ago defies the odds. Your pain is the only visible indication of it. We need to figure out why you're only experiencing pain." He pulled the sheet and blanket up on me a little.

"That's good, I guess."

"The good news is, we can manage that. Someone is coming to bring the medications. The good news is I think the antiviral is strong enough to help slow the pain attacks it just takes a while for it to work–.."

"I saw that other vial you now have in your pocket, doctor." I cut him off. The pain was still somewhat wrenching but I wanted to get my point across.

"Let's say you take these restraints off and I won't tell the next person that comes in here to check your pockets." I looked him square in the eyes with my best poker face. He spoke only after he narrowed his eyes at me and took a deep breath of his own.

"Seanna, you fail to understand. I'm not the one in charge of making the decision to remove your restraints. You're incorrect if you think telling on me will increase your chances of getting out of this room or seeing your loved ones and boyfriend again. If you were able to recall my first name then I'm sure you can remember what I told you the last time we spoke." He was calm and serious in his reply as his dark eyes stared at me right back.

Touché, doctor. Touché.

I took a moment in my now subsiding pain and thought about what he said. The doctor could see that I was mulling this over as the door opened again and the same man from before returned with a partially filled, small syringe and a two hundred –fifty cubic centimeter fluid bag of the anti–viral, I assume. He gave the two items to the doctor who placed the bag on the IV pole for later and took the syringe and started to administer the drug into the IV port, same as before. I noticed the man resumed his post observing as the doctor quietly finished the injection. In that short amount of time, I'd change my mind about receiving the pain medication– it was now a Godsend because by now I was exhausted from going through intense spasms of pain that radiated everywhere from head to toe.

"What time is it?" I asked before what I found out was Dilaudid made me not care.

"It's late. But not too late for you, Seanna," He winked at me without a smile, turn-ed around and both of the men walked out of the room. Damn him and his coded speech. The truth was I felt I was probably no better off here than on my own apart from receiving this wonderful blessing of pain medication– which I could also more than likely get on my own, I think. Who the hell was he to say he could help me? He was no more than a few years older than me and seemingly farther down the chain of command than a janitor at a Fortune five–hundred company according to his 'I told you, I'm not the one in charge,' statement.

As I lay there about to drift off again, I promised myself I would stay on track and do whatever I could to find out about this virus in me and the whereabouts of my boy-friend. It wasn't fair for them to keep me against my will without allowing for at least some communication with Graham. If I were in a jail I'd at least get a phone call. If I heard him correctly, he mentioned he could help me get to my family too. I realized then, just how did he know about my family or if I even had any family left? I don't re-member speaking of them and the only person I told Dr. Chaven I came into contact with was Graham. I tried to sit up at the realization but the effects from medication took over and it now felt like I was glued to the bed. The dim lighting in the room was no help as the darkness in the room blurred into the light that was only closest around the bed and the monitors. The machines beeped more at a normal frequency as their sound now echoed as if they were in a cave.

Who was this doctor? Where in the state of New Jersey was I? There went my consciousness, again.

I wish I could say I woke up back in my own bed. Truth be told, I wished for a lot of things, like last month when dead people remained inanimate objects after their time was up. I woke up to the same surroundings except there was a now a tray table sitt-ing off to the side that had a covered dish alongside a pitcher and glass with the usual silverware. Finally the hospitality arrived. My whole body from head to toe was aching and sore beyond belief. I could only liken it to the way your leg hurts after a severe muscle cramp, only it was everywhere. I instinctively ran my fingers through my hair noticing first how they got stuck in a tangle by the time they were no more than a few inches from my head. My light brown hair was well past my shoulders and took more of my mother's African American thickness versus my father's thinner, British strands. It took me only a half second to realize my newly granted freedom in the absence of the restraints. I couldn't see myself but imagine my eyes lit up before the feeling of soreness brought me back to reality. I still had the IV in my arm as I sat straight up in the bed. I carefully lifted my right arm bending it to reach to my back left shoulder, checking for the bullet wound— which was still there and noticeable by the bandage but not overly painful considering how I felt everywhere else.

I was only a few seconds into my discovery when the door opened again and Dr. Chavan walked in. Does this guy ever rest?

"I see you're up. Good morning!" he said in the most pleasant tone I'd heard from him yet.

"Yes, I am. The restraints are off— thank you." I replied.

I wanted to be sure he understood my gratitude because the only thing that's worse than being bed-ridden is to be bedridden by force. Being a paramedic, even I saw the difference in the behaviors of people who found themselves restrained for whatever reason. Restraints often make people want to resist, plain and simple. I would be no different.

The doctor walked alongside the bed and took a good look at me before doing the same at the monitors, seemingly satisfied with what he saw. I told him how sore I was and he performed a quick neurological exam saying it was necessary in order for me to be able to move around and walk— and also to be sure the spasms were the cause of the soreness and not something else. He also told me that they'd be doing another MRI later on today, though I didn't remember the first one. I remembered the promise I made to myself to be as inquisitive as possible because aside from whatever goals they had for me, I had goals of my own. Dr. Chavan along with everyone else here were no dummies so I know I'd have to be genuine, otherwise I'd get nowhere. I decided I'd ask some indirect questions before getting to the root of my concerns.

"So, can I ask you doctor, how did the restraints end up coming off?"

I could tell he was thinking carefully about his every word. "Well, that other guy that was in here with me is one of many people here working on this, your acquired illness. He came in with me to observe you a little and after many tests in the lab and our meeting this morning it was decided that you're not high risk."

"High risk? For what?" I asked.

"Well, there are several factors that must be considered, Seanna. What we can see from you, since you are confirmed infected. Behaviorally, you are not where others in the population with the disease are. You're responsive and normal with no degenerative symptoms. Physiologically, your vitals are only slightly elevated– which even those are slowly returning to acceptable ranges. The lab results– which are always last to confirm, are significant because on a cellular level your blood samples are responding in a way that shows us that others will not be at risk should they become exposed." He took a minute to let it all sink in but all I could think about was that extra blood sample he took but never turned over to the other man for testing.

"So, you're saying, I have the virus, but I don't . . . respond to it?" I know by now I was looking as confused as the question implied.

"Yes and no," he replied. I could already see the reflective answer coming from within him.

"What I'm implying is, under the current regiment of large doses of antivirals and antibiotic, your infection could possibly be controlled, though not cured. It doesn't look as if it will be fatal to you." There was no enthusiasm at all for what seemed like very good news to me.

"Great! That's good news then, right?" I was beginning to be elated. That was the best news I'd heard in days, I think. For some reason I didn't know yet, the doctor sat there at the foot of the bed, motionless and looked at the floor. I knew I was about to find out why he wasn't celebrating my miracle with me. My smile faded before he spoke again.

"Seanna, for reasons right or wrong the authorities have decided the best course of action for dealing with infected people is to– . . . " He wouldn't say it.

I would though. "Kill them, I know."

"Right, the military and law enforcement have been given orders to shoot on sight anyone they believe to be infected under the Rule of Two." he stopped knowing I wouldn't know what he was talking about.

"All they need is for two people to agree that a person is infected before it is considered justified. These officers and soldiers are trained to move quickly in small teams, there is not much debate," he explained.

"So?" I replied.

"On the outside things appear normal, but no one knows what will happen without treatment, if you miss a dose or worse– your status becomes known by others? Or better yet, say they're able to kill or contain every infected person, do you think they'll risk another outbreak by allowing you to return to a normal setting?"

Despite the admission he was kind enough to let it sink in for a minute. There was an abundant silence between us as I sat there reflecting on what was said. I tried to put on a brave face but there was not a whole lot of reason to be brave right now– it felt like the world I was a part of was now pushing me away from it. I was told my life no longer had value in the sense that I had what every live person wanted eradicated off the planet. I was being voided.

I sat there looking pitiful for a moment longer, with my gown partially slumped off of one shoulder. I cleared my throat to speak, though I didn't know what I would say.

"What should I do?" I said. It was the best I could come up with.

"Fortunately, someone you know likes you enough to invest a lot of effort into keeping you secret and out of harm's way. You'll be talking to them directly in a little while. In the meantime, procedurally, now that you're conscious we'll have you sign consent forms for the treatment and care that you're receiving. I'm working with a select number of patients to see if perhaps through you, a vaccine can be made," he revealed in a tone that could've sounded more reassuring.

"What should I do?" I repeated.

"I would strongly suggest that you sign all of the forms."

"If it isn't too soon, can I take shower? I think I'd feel much better." I asked.

He got up and said he'd send someone in here to help me and that he'd be back in a few hours. I had no choice but to sit there as the machines did their monitoring. Dr. Chavan left without another word. I looked over at the tray table not hungry for anything on it but instead using it as a focal point. It took only a few seconds longer before the tears welled up and started to run down my cheeks. The enormity of what was going on and my worrying about so many people at the same moment all came to me in a blur of memories. I leaned over from the bed to grab the box of tissues from the nightstand when the door opened and a woman walked in. The woman, a nurse, I presume, was taller than me, of medium build with long straight hair that was half blonde and half gray. She also wore purple scrubs with matching clogs and looked as if she'd been in the nursing field since I'd been alive. She saw my mood and gave me a half crooked little smile– the kind meant purely for pity.

"Hello Seanna, my name is Laura. I'm here to help you shower and eat," she said in a plain, seemingly scripted tone.

I don't know what she knew about me or if she drew the short straw but she was cautious. Laura paused and then walked over to the bed with some waterproof band-ages in her hand. She put some latex gloves on and started disconnecting the IV and turned the machines off as they responded to the interruption. She worked quickly as she wrapped my IV ports and wounds with the bandage then reached in the drawer and grabbed a pair of footies and handed them to me. I put them on as best as I could as she apparently laid down the rules.

"I have some of the antiviral, if needed. The showers are close to your room but I was instructed that you shouldn't take more than twenty minutes. I can stand in there with you, if you need me to or not- if you're uncomfortable but I cannot leave you completely alone. You have to agree that you will let me know immediately if you feel like something's wrong or you're in pain again, do you understand?" She rhythmically blurted.

After acknowledging her request with a simple nod, I slowly stood up- my knees feeling sore, weak and wobbly. For a quick second it felt like they were going to give out and Laura reached to help but quickly looked as if she regretted doing so. Not caring about how much my gown was open in the back I began to walk toward the door with Laura at my side. Speaking of, I didn't know what was on the other side of the door- if there were going to be many people there or if there was a big open space with windows or if it was enclosed amongst many hallways and doors. I was going to be observant and try and see if there was anything that would be helpful in getting to Graham- even if this was only a trip to the bathroom.

Laura took a few quick steps and opened the door for me. The area outside of the room was brighter than what I was used to, so my eyes had to adjust. Once I could see more clearly, the immediate space looked more like an office building with plenty of off-white colored walls and an occasional framed picture of various woodland scenes that were evenly spaced every fifteen feet in between doors and such. I discovered the room I came out of was toward the end of the hallway with a realistic looking nurses' station nearby that had all of the similar monitors I had in my room. I figured they must be linked because the screens were dark just like the ones in the room were now. There were two people, a man and a woman sitting behind the counter and at the desk. When the woman saw me, she whispered quickly to the man whose back was toward me. He immediately turned around to look. Could they be any more conspicuous? I gave them an undeserved crooked little smile before looking down the long hallway trying to guess which door could possibly be the bathroom. The nurse Laura told the two gawkers that we'd be back shortly, to get someone up to change the sheets and that she would call with the lunch orders for everyone once she returned. She looked at me for a brief moment before she spat out a quick, "Do you have any food allergies?" I shook my head 'no' and she proceeded to walk a few steps in front of me until we were three doors down then she stopped. She reached into her pocket, got out keys for the door and unlocked it. I felt uneasy as I could sense the two sets of eyes on my backside all the way from the station.

"I can't wait until they get the electronic card readers on this floor. This is annoying carrying keys around everywhere," she complained as she jiggled the fussy knob and opened the door for me. She looked down at her watch and informed me, "You have fifteen minutes, try not to get those bandages too soaked, there's shampoo and soap on the counter there by the towels- those folded clothes over there should fit you- if not, we can find you some in another size."

"Got it," I replied.

"I'll grab a chair and be right outside the door."

I answered again before I walked in and shut the door behind me. I hoped for a lock on the inside but was disappointed to find nothing but a blank metal panel that was round enough for where the lock should've been. The beige colored bathroom was sectioned off into three areas; a sink with a large counter and mirror, the toilet area and lastly the shower which I went to first to turn the water on so it would be warm enough by the time I stepped in. The space looked newly remodeled so it didn't seem as if it would take long at all before it was at a good temperature. After relieving myself I was eager to find a comb and all the things Laura pointed out to me. By then, I figured I now had less than twelve minutes to wash my hair and body.

As the water from the shower made a splashing sound from hitting the dark blue tile floor, I worked quickly and as delicately as possible combing my hair until it was smooth and without tangles– regrettably, my left arm was of no use because it hurt too much to lift it more than a few inches away from my side. I realized I must've taken a few minutes so I slipped off my gown, stepped into the shower stream and let the hot water run through my hair and shoulders– screw Laura's warnings about a soaked bandage! I was busy enough trying to create a lather with the shampoo and clean as much of my body as possible because I wasn't sure if she had the go–ahead to drag me out of the bathroom if I took longer than permitted. The soap and water felt good on me and was the first bit of comfort I'd felt in a while. The hot steam and the sound of the water was what I focused on because it was just like home. After I washed all of the important parts I focused on my hair again and closed my eyes letting the shampoo and soap wash away completely.

"All right, it's almost time to go back." Laura opened the door and said it with authority.

"Okay, I'm finished." I said though now I suddenly felt like I was in jail. Having to return back to a room where I would spend my day without the choice of coming or going– it seemed like nothing but incarceration. Laura closed the door again and the cool air from the hallway brushed in giving me chills that caused a slight shiver. I turned the water off, bent over to twist my hair out of water to the best of my ability. I grabbed a towel to wrap it in because I doubt I'd be given extra time for vanity reasons. I used another towel to dry off with– quickly as I could with one good hand, getting just barely dry enough for the Hanes cotton under ware and medium sized dark blue pants that looked more like a thicker version of hospital scrubs. There was a white short-sleeved button–up shirt folded there, that I took my time getting into because my back was still a little wet. Laura opened the door again but I was ready enough so I wouldn't have to hear her complain about taking too long. While she came back in and collected my old gown I picked up the other toiletries like the deodorant, comb and lotion that were lying on the counter because I'd prefer not to skimp on those necessities. She gave me a somewhat frustrated look as I said, "I know, I'm coming," before she could say another word.

As we walked back down the hallway there was a cleaning cart outside my room already. The two gawkers from earlier were busy standing by a fax machine and copier chatting about something but I couldn't hear what they were talking about. When they saw us the woman put a little stack of papers inside of a manila folder, got Laura's attention and handed it to her. When I stepped inside of the room I saw the sheets had been changed and two extra pillows had been added. I hadn't a clue as to whom it belonged to but there was a nice looking handmade quilt, folded so that it covered the lower half of the bed. I was thankful that someone attempted to make me feel at home though I was sure that everyone in the building could use a little something that reminded them of better times. I didn't know for sure which loved ones I'd lost but I knew that these people were here working to help save the lives of those they could— even though they've probably lost some family and friends too.

Working off to the side of the room's entry, I was able to see the person responsible for my tidied room. It was a short, middle-aged, African American man. He was thin with glasses and had slightly graying, thick hair. Given the circumstances, he was pleasant— I could tell because as he turned to empty the trash— he saw me and said, "Well, there she is!" in a friendly tone as if I were someone he knew already. Now facing me, I could see his name sewn on the patch on the upper left side of his work shirt. The name 'Ruben' was written in typical white cursive. He walked right up to me with a genuine smile, nodded his head and then went on with what he was doing but not before exchanging more pleasantries. By far, his greeting was the kindest.

"So you're the one they have in this room with no furnishings, no entertainment, no nothing?" he joked as he tossed the small bag of trash past us and into the hallway by his cart. I didn't know what to say especially since I didn't know that furniture was an option.

"Entertainment is not a priority for her right now," Laura motioned for me to get back in the bed. I did, knowing not to press my luck on these feelings of wellness. Once I was sitting back on the bed, she started removing the shower bandages. I heard her sighs, disapproving of the moisture that got in. Ruben kept working, wiping the tray table down and pressed on with the issue about my solitary confinement.

"You're a pretty young woman— you look about my niece's age. I bet you listen to that R&B and Hip-Hop, don't you?" he continued.

"Yes sir, but I like a little bit of everything," I informed him kindly.

"Uh-huh, just like my niece. Well, there ought to be a radio 'round here somewhere— and some CDs with something you'd like to listen to— I'll check around and see." Ruben replaced the nearly empty box of tissues with a new one before he turned to leave.

"Ruben, thank you for the quilt and pillows," I said before he was gone.

"You're welcome sweetheart, take care," he replied as he closed the door.

Laura finished reattaching the IV, blood pressure cuff, and the oxygen sensor, looked at her watch and said, "I'll bring your lunch in shortly— it'll be chicken noodle soup with toast and ginger ale or clear soda— something light since you're on a couple of medications."

"How are you feeling? Are you in any pain?" She questioned further.

"Just a little concerned from being shot in the shoulder, bitten on the arm and not knowing exactly where I am." I told her flatly. She had that coming.

I could tell she didn't appreciate my reaction because her eyes narrowed and she simply replied, "Okay— understandable," as she turned around to get the manila folder from the chair seat and handed it to me. "You need to read through these and sign wherever you see the 'X' is highlighted. I'll be back with a pen and your food." With that, Laura left my room. I'm sure she was in love with the idea of being my nurse due to her attitude toward me the whole time.

Laura returned after a few minutes as promised with the tray and its contents containing exactly what she described was for lunch, along with a pen. I hadn't yet opened the manila folder to read anything because I'd just finished putting on the deodorant, lotion and was now slowly combing through my hair to help it dry, as best as I could with one good arm. After she moved the tray table close and put the food on it, she walked out without a word— which was okay with me, I knew what I had to do. The smell of the soup caught my attention so I started in on it first. It only took a few spoonfuls before I felt full but managed to drink some of the ginger ale.

Feeling satisfied enough, I moved the table out of the way so I could look at the papers I had to sign. It was a good thing I wasn't left handed because I saw at least ten highlighted X's requiring a signature. Some of the papers were medical release forms, permission and acknowledgement of treatment forms, release of liability forms and a general patient information form that I was surprised to find already filled out with my name, address, driver's license, social security number, height, weight and hair color pre-printed in black in all of the appropriate places. The only thing missing was a wallet sized photo. I didn't think much beyond it since most of the medical records had recently become electronic. It couldn't have been too hard to get the information as most of the regional hospitals use the same database. As far as I skimmed, everything seemed pretty cut and dry using standard terms. At the top of most of the forms I saw in printed letterhead 'NGT Labs, Inc.' which was completely unfamiliar to me. I'd never heard of NGT and its suggestion that I wasn't in an actual hospital receiving care. For the emergency contact I was hesitant but listed my parents since Graham was already here. I wrote down their phone number hoping they'd have more luck than I did if they needed to be called. After I finished signing the last document I put the neat little stack back into the manila folder and sat it on the tray table.

Out of curiosity, I started poking around the bandage on my forearm, slowly peeling back the tape that I found had a pretty decent adhesive in my opinion. I was curious to see the bite mark once again because it was the reason my fate had swung in such a sad and unusual direction. Apparently, because of some reason unknown to me, I was no longer a candidate for death— an option previously not yet available to anyone else in the same scenario. Slowly revealing the scar, I bent my arm to look more closely. The scar line was crooked but was healing. I pulled the bandage completely off— letting it fall on the bed. I touched the sutured wound, ever so gently. It was still tender and red but not yet bruised like I'd seen in other injuries. Also, there was the absence of mucous build-up. I tugged a little at the tiny sutures that sprung out like overgrown hairs but regretted doing so as it resulted in a stinging sensation at the site. A few seconds later, Dr. Chavan walked in.

"It probably wasn't a good idea to remove that, yet." He said as he approached me, looking directly at my arm.

"I can't help it— I had to see." I responded, trying not to sound like a whiny little child. "Besides, I'm a paramedic and I'm just as curious about injuries as you, doctor." I said in attempt to make myself sound more reasonable.

"Laura mentioned that you might be in pain, do you need some more medication right now?" he said.

"Honestly, I'm feeling a little better than before. I'm just worried about my family and I'd like to speak with someone here who can tell me where my boyfriend is— he needs to know I'm not dead or dying."

"We know, Seanna. Can you try and raise your left arm for me? As high as you can," he instructed.

"Doctor, you're not going to get me to do anything right now but inquire about my loved ones. Where's Graham? I know someone here knows where he is," I was beginning to become a little irritated now as I got up from the bed, faster than he expected. I didn't know what I was going to do— if I'd thought about it longer I would've kept my mouth shut and raised my arm like he asked. The doctor took a step back but oddly I could sense that it wasn't in fear of me or my actions. Knowing that the IV would limit my outburst, I disconnected it while Dr. Chavan simply said, "Seanna, think about what you're doing, you're being irrational. Remember what I told you?" He held his arms out, palms facing me in a reassuring effort to slow my commotion.

"If I can't get an answer from you, I guess I'll have to find someone who has them. I know my rights. I'm ending my treatment as of now!" I replied. I was nearly barefoot in footies but I marched right past him without interference to the door, opened it and walked out into the hallway. The same two staff members from before were at the station when they looked up and became visibly nervous after they saw me walk out unescorted. The male quickly picked the phone and dialed a few numbers, which was perfect; they could call me a cab out of there as far as I was concerned. Dr. Chavan came right out and tried to reassure the two whose eyes never left me. "It's okay, calm down. She just wants to see her boyfriend— that's all," he said quickly and turned his focus back to me.

"Which way is the exit?" I yelled out to anyone within earshot. I looked closely to see if any one of them would unintentionally look toward a door and give the exit away. My theory was correct because the woman behind the desk quickly looked past me, down the hallway nearby where the bathroom was located. Instead of the right hand side I figured it would be on the interior side of the building. Good– thank you, I thought, as I turned around and started walking down the hall. The man behind the desk said out loud, "I've got security on the line!" before he mumbled a few words into the phone. Dr. Chavan and now Laura– who likely heard the commotion and came to see, followed closely behind. I didn't run, but I walked quickly and purposefully toward the section of hallway which was near the bathroom I used earlier. It didn't take but a half-second to look up and see the red 'Exit' sign. I thanked God for building codes and required fire exit routes as I opened the door to the stairwell and started down the stairs. The stairwell was light yellow, well lit and noticeably colder by the hard floor underneath my feet in contrast to the carpeting elsewhere. I held on to the railing as I went down one flight and then another. I must've been on the fifth floor because there was a visible, numerical 'three' sign by the doorway of the next floor down. I kept going. I heard the doctor's and Laura's footsteps about a flight of stairs behind me and as I rounded the second floor and kept on to the next one. I looked at them and smirked after the doctor called out, "You aren't going to see your boyfriend this way– in fact, you're going to get yourself killed, please just come back to the room with me Seanna." I didn't break my stride –I just replied, "I am of sound mind doctor, I am checking myself out now."

I got to the first floor doorway, made eye contact with the doctor one more time before rolling my eyes in defiance and opened the door. I stepped into a hallway that in my opinion was beautifully furnished with obviously more expensive décor featuring a dark silver metallic, executive theme. It was a stark difference from the makeshift hospital floor that I just came from upstairs that would totally pass on a movie set. I made it a few steps before the doctor and company got out of stairwell and continued behind me at a safe distance. I didn't have a clue which way to go but I knew the building exit had to be somewhere. Maybe they'd have an information desk with a map where there would be a 'You are here' sign and the entrance clearly marked for visitors. I'd just rounded the corner when I saw him again. Our eyes met and I knew instantly who he was from our brief encounter at Graham's house. Those blue eyes focused right into mine like the bullet that went into my shoulder– they were piercing. I stopped immediately in an attempt to keep some space between us– which wasn't more than fifteen feet. He was tall, well past six feet and dressed in the same type of uniform as before; leading me to think that he was security for the facility. To make things worse, he was carrying an automatic rifle. Two more men dressed in the same attire arrived from down the hallway, rushing to join him at each side. I'd say that not even the world's best running back would get through them to the other side now. I quickly looked behind me as three additional uniformed men with guns ran up to join Dr. Chavan and Laura who now were just a few yards away from me as well. I was completely cornered now. My heart was ready to race out of my chest, though I doubt with the guns surrounding me– it would make it far either.

Blue eyes, although I couldn't be sure that he was the only blue-eyed person here amongst the growing crowd, raised his weapon at me and calmly stated, "Which will it be Seanna- room or body bag?"

I didn't look at anyone except him. They all had weapons but his was pointed at my head and commanded all of my attention. I was more afraid now than ever before since the doctor informed me of the Rule of Two which meant that only one other person was needed to justify my being killed. Point blank- no further questions asked.

Did my life really mean so little now?

"This is bull shit! I'm not trying to hurt anyone- I just want to get out of here!" I yelled.

"Everything is okay, Seanna misunderstands her situation and just needs an escort back to her room. Mr. Davenport this doesn't need to get out of hand." Dr. Chavan spoke loudly from around the corner for him to hear.

So, Mr. Davenport was his name. He never took his blue eyes off of me. Instead he just remained still and focused on his target.

"Mr. Davenport, I- I don't know what's going on but I've already been shot before- I know you all mean business. I need to get to my family, that's all I want." I pleaded with him to the best of my ability.

"You are infected. There are only two choices for you. I stated them already." he replied coldly as he readied the firearm. There was a slight clicking sound to confirm. Even with so many in the hallway, it was so quiet now you could probably hear an ant hiccup. The silence was broken by a radio from one of the armed guards, where the person on the other end was inquiring about the situation. The man who wore the radio was standing next to Davenport and responded quietly with, "We have her now- containment in progress."

I tried not to let them see me look but there was only one door in hallway closest to where I was. There was no way I'd be able to make it before Davenport put a round or two in my head. I didn't know if there was anything else to do because it seemed he was determined to kill me. Therefore in my mind, I only had one other choice. The break I desperately needed came from farther down the hallway Davenport had come from- another door, when it opened again. Two individuals in lab coats quickly approached the three. It was a man and a woman who yelled, "Do not shoot her!" when she saw the gun aimed at me. Davenport turned his head only slightly and that was my cue to go for the door. I don't even know if it was unlocked but I had to try because there wasn't any other place to go. Everyone sprang into motion went they saw me move. I extended my arm to open the door and was surprised to find it was unlocked. The security team closed in quickly as I stepped in and turned to slam the door slut. I had additional luck because of a standard knob lock that I quickly turned. Less than a second later they made it to the door because the knob twisted but did not open.

I had to be in someone's office because of the way it was furnished but all I cared about was the window and possible exit it provided. I ran to the window but was out of time to do much else before the door knob exploded from a gunshot. The door violently swung open from a kick and Davenport with a handgun this time stepped in, aimed right at me and took a shot.

"No— don't!" was all I could plead before I felt the impact. To my surprise I was not pierced from a bullet this time, but instead a dart had imbedded itself in my right shoulder. Are these even legal? Davenport stood in the doorway watching, seemingly satisfied with his shot. Within seconds I felt my vision blur and my legs give out as I fell to the floor. I laid there like I was stunned. and I could tell that most of the people from the hallway came into the room but all who was in my view was Davenport and the dark haired woman with the lab coat who came by my side and checked me.

"Get her back upstairs into a secured room this time. Sainiraj, you're filling out the report on this one. Be sure and write down it's your own damn fault!" the woman spoke sternly.

Davenport stood over me as I tried to stay awake, yet again. I was only able to mumble a faint, "Get away from me," as I was completely paralyzed and almost unconscious when he bent over and scooped me up. I wanted to resist, to rebel, or at the very least spit in his face to let him know how much I hated him— but those thoughts floated right away with my consciousness.

CHAPTER SIX

Waking up in an unfamiliar place can be stressful enough on its own. Waking up with the last memory of being shot at prior to being swarmed by a room full of strangers only to wake up in another strange place is the ultimate form of humility. This has happened to me twice now. All of a sudden, my life goes from mundane with the source of my excitement coming from my line of work as a paramedic to a full-on, 'Who-the-heck-knows what will happen next with a high chance of mortality being a constant'. In my mind I could still see those piercing blue eyes that wanted me dead.

I woke up on a couch that was made of leather. It was cold but plush as it cradled around my body which was curled up and covered with a simple throw. I had the same clothes on as before and could still even smell the lotion I applied shortly before I unsuccessfully tried to leave. After all that went on I was now in a nice office- an executive suite it had to be because there was another couch separate from a desk space that might as well had a sign hanging above it that says, "*CEO sits here*". Everything in the room was dark and rich in color from the mahogany wood on the desk to the high back chairs across from it to the carpets and matching couch set that I was curled up on. I could tell it was all very tastefully chosen in the absence of a budget or the need for a sale price. I took a few seconds sitting up, still feeling lightheaded from the dart that was now causing some soreness in my right upper chest area. It didn't take long for me to see the huge window behind the desk so I slowly got up to walk over there first instead of trying for the door which I figured would be locked anyway. I noticed I still had no shoes on.

The window gave me my first glance into the outside world which was from about six stories up, I would guess. I didn't know where I was or if I was in the same building as before because I had less than a second to see out of the last window before the door got kicked in and I was down on the floor. The view I had now was just barely above the treetops where everything looked peaceful and serene. As far as I could see there was nothing but greenery and mature trees. There were even a few Eastern Bluebirds perched on a branch of one of the trees nearby. I looked back over at the desk which was kept neat and tidy, there were no papers lying in sight. The computer monitor was off and there wasn't a logo or business name anywhere. On a side table there was a jar of peppermints along with some common houseplants, one them being of the *Pothos* variety. I knew it was because I had one in my apartment.

Seeing the phone on the desk, I immediately thought about calling Graham's cell phone but I doubt he would've had the chance to take it with him amidst all of the commotion that took place before we were escorted from his house. I decided to try anyway. Picking up the phone, I started dialing the first few numbers of the area code when the office door opened ever so slightly and in walked a familiar face. I hung up the phone and had to blink a few times. It was my uncle Lloyd, my father's older brother and a man I'd not seen in years. He was dressed sharply with a dark grey shirt, black slacks and a grey and silver striped tie. Though he was slightly shorter, he shared the same hairline and nose as my father.

"Uncle Lloyd?" I said with an upward inflection.

"Yes, my niece– it's me," he replied as he smiled, walked over to me and gave me a long and hearty hug. He was the first family I'd seen or heard from in days. I rested easy for a moment before a cluster of questions came to my mind. My tears beat me to anything as they streamed down my face. Sensing all of this, he pat my back softly until I let go and backed away. "I've spoken to your mother and my brother, rest assured they are alive," he spoke again.

"Oh thank God!" I exhaled. "I tried to call them once I found out what was going on but all I could do was leave a message. Have you heard from–," he knew right away I was referring to my own brother and remained solemn as he shook his head and replied, "We will double back and check for him again, soon. Here, sit down," he said as he directed me back to the couch.

"Is this virus thing everywhere?" I said as I followed his direction and sat down almost exactly in the spot where I woke up from as the spot was still warm. Uncle Lloyd went to a cabinet, opened it and took out a box of tissues. He sat down next to me before he started filling me in.

"I'm sorry to tell you this, but yes, it is mostly everywhere. Officials and many others cooperating tried their best to hold it off for as long as they could. It's been nearly a week since it surfaced and many, many people are dead and missing. There are also many people in hiding and I hope that's the case with your brother." He looked at me very carefully with full eye contact.

"It's like a dream, like fiction. I can't believe how quickly things have gotten out of hand." I said, looking out at the peaceful treetops from my view of the window.

"Unfortunately, it's not a dream, Seanna. It came to be this way simply because no one ever expected something like this. You're safe here, first and foremost, you understand? I know it's been a rough time for you. There's a lot going on and a lot you may not yet realize or know but you'll come to understand in a short while." He calmly explained.

I could tell he was noting my every movement and reaction as he looked down at my left arm. I had so many things I wanted to know– it would be impossible to rank them in priority. Just because I was safe meant nothing if my family and the general population, were not.

"Are you a part of this?" I said as I looked around me referring to the research center "Is this where you work?" I continued on.

"I've been here doing research on various projects for years, your father was aware of that– which is why I haven't seen most of the family in a while. After the divorce was finalized there was nothing left for me to do but work. Nathan went off to college and Melanie took half of everything," he said, smiling a little.

My uncle and his wife Melanie divorced about seven years ago after twenty-four years of marriage. Lloyd was always a workaholic and shortly after their youngest of two, my cousin Paige died in a hit and run accident, just weeks after her fifteenth birthday, Lloyd buried himself further into his work and Melanie was never the same. She still calls my mother occasionally and sends a Christmas card every year. I was just two years older than Paige when she died. I remember it being so sudden and tragic because the four of us Nathan, Paige, myself and my brother Junior all got along well. Her accidental death was part of the reason I chose to become a paramedic.

He continued on, "While our focus was on several projects regarding research for cancer fighting medications in the nineties as well as for drug therapies to preserve life at the cellular level, some time ago we were presented with a unique opportunity to begin looking into cellular regeneration, much like the anti aging regiments sold over the counter these days. In order to stay in the competitive ranks and continue to be funded adequately we had to shift our focus a little. The company I worked for merged with another laboratory and we've since merged yet again. Through countless hours of hard work and achievement I've been fortunate enough to advance myself and I am now in charge of this division," he spoke pointedly as if he were being an interviewed for an article in *Popular Science* magazine.

I couldn't help but think of my Aunt Melanie's description of all of this which I overheard through countless hours of conversations with my mother about how my uncle missed most of the achievements made by his own children and how his absence turned into guilt after Paige died. They were always well to do and it was easy to see his achievements materialize into things like second homes, expensive cars and social clubs; none of which Melanie wanted at the price of his absence. She just wanted her husband after a normal eight hour workday.

"I heard of your successes through the years," I replied.

"Indeed. All that you see here is a result of decades of steady progress and many sacrifices including my own marital content. You are alive now because of it," he said as he referred to my arm again.

"Speaking of, how am I still alive?" I interrupted.

"That's a long story that will require your complete attention and cooperation again as it's probably time for more medication now," he said as he looked at the clock on the wall, stood up and walked to the door. He opened it ever so slightly to talk to someone on the other side and said, "I'll take those meds now, thank you." A few seconds later Lloyd was handed a few syringes which he closed the door back and returned to where I was seated. He placed the syringes on the end table where I could clearly see them. He sat next to me.

"The contents in those syringes are responsible for your continued survival- your life," he stated simply.

"The anti-viral, right?" I questioned, because I assumed nothing at this point.

"Yes along with pain medications and some valium, just to help prevent agitation," he tried to assure me. "The antiviral has been specially made to fit your needs- though it is not a cure."

I couldn't help but be a little suspicious. "The valium is not here to make me more compliant, is it? Because that's what I think of when it comes to valium," I eyed him intently waiting for his response.

"No, my dear, it's not like that at all. The people in the lab are trying to figure out all of the symptoms associated with your condition. Agitation is a common symptom for most any serious ailment and anything I can do to make you more comfortable, I will. It's the least I can do," he responded casually.

I waited as Lloyd paused, then grabbed the first of the three syringes. He softly patted the side of my arm and said, "These can go right in your arm, about every four hours or so, okay?"

"Alright."

Without gloves, he started the injections one after another and told me that my arm would be a little sore- this was the least of my worries though. I've had enough pain for three sore arms so far. Once he finished he carefully replaced the tips on the needles and took the empty syringes to the door where he opened it and handed it off to the person on the other side for disposal. I wasn't surprised there wasn't a sharps container in the office because, well, why would there be? Lloyd told me to relax a little and offered me water to drink- which I accepted. Feeling the effects from the pain reliever and the valium I rested my head back on the couch and closed my eyes for a few seconds. It wasn't long before someone knocked at the door again which startled and awakened me from my temporary respite. My uncle Lloyd quickly went to the door again and exchanged more dialog and was back near my side within a minute.

"How are you feeling my dear?" He asked, seeming honestly concerned.

"I feel a little lightheaded but I'm okay- considering everything." I decided to probe a little further into the earlier events of the day. Maybe a little less inhibition was one of the side effects from the valium. I decided I would give it a try. "Uncle, I know they informed you of what happened earlier today. Would they have killed me if they had no other option?" I asked. As if he knew the question was coming he stared down at the floor as he contemplated his answer.

"What we're dealing with is something serious, Seanna. I believe the plague of the dark ages will soon be shadowed by this event. The same day you came here one of our own employees and their family member– both of whom were unknowingly afflict- ed from the slightest contact, managed to get through and set up residence here despite our aggressive and repeated testing procedures. While there are no guidelines for this kind of situation– everyone who could get here, showed up– regardless of our request that only non–afflicted employees report in. We had to tell dozens of our own to go to the local hospitals instead. In hindsight, it was to be expected. People want the opportunity to save their own lives and while I can't say I blame them– it cost us dear- ly. Those people who were once alive and are now roaming the streets committing these atrocities acts and gaining numbers have no will of their own anymore." He pau- sed for a few seconds before giving me the short and final answer.

"I apologize for the extreme measures they took; however, if those officers had determined your will was gone, *yes*."

I wasn't surprised by his confirmation. By now I was beginning to not take it per- sonally anymore. After what I experienced earlier with Darin I would probably volunteer for the firing squad myself if things went sour. Lloyd spoke up and tried his best to smooth things over and said, "I know they seemed a bit forceful but trust me they had only been through a similar scenario earlier with a more deadly conclusion."

"I hate to sound like a broken record but I only wanted to see Graham and not just hear from someone that he was okay. I want to see both him and my parents." I reasoned with him.

"You will, Seanna. They're anxious to see for themselves that you are okay. I will report to them myself after I've finished getting you settled in and tell them that you are doing well. In the meanwhile, I have decided to change your room to somewhere a little more comfortable so you won't feel so . . . "

"Incarcerated," I finished his sentence coming up with my own perfect description.

"Yes, right," he chuckled. "It'll be more acceptable to you– I think." He went to the door where he opened it again and requested a wheelchair which I told him that I wanted to walk. He didn't seem too surprised by my request for independence, though it was more for my own dignity. The men doing security probably wanted me in the chair because in order for me to rebel or escape I would have to get out of it first, which would give them some extra time to react. After a second or two of contem- plation my uncle agreed it would be okay. He helped me to stand up and cautiously escorted me through the office door. Once we were out of the office we walked into a hallway that was the similar to the hallway from earlier. The valium must've started to work because I no longer felt offended by the presence of the extra people around us. I saw two armed men standing outside the immediate area and another at the elevator just yards away– no sign of Davenport though. I was still without shoes and would've gladly walked all the way there as such but by the time we got into the elevator and down to the ground level there was someone there with shoes in hand for me to put on.

It seemed highly likely that by now certain NGT employees knew every little minute detail about me– down to whether or not I had shoes on, which was kind of scary, if not intrusive. Once the shoes were on I noticed the security escort had grown by two more officers which brought the count up to five. Two officers led me and my uncle and three were only a step behind us. I thought about what might happen to me if I so much as jumped suddenly and yelled "*boo!*" It must've been the valium again in my mind, helping me find another way to wind up getting shot again. I also wondered now if we were in the same building as before because of the same colored walls and decorative plants in the corner.

"Am I being moved to a different building?" I asked as my curiosity overrode my silence.

My uncle leaned closer into me as he said, "Yes, we're going to a different building this time. It's more secure but you will also have a few more amenities." He put his arm around my shoulder like we were old pals or something but I figured it was his attempt to comfort me and to show the few people in the hallway by the entrance that he was supportive and that I wasn't an animal.

The entrance was surrounded by thick glass walls. The sun was shining still, though making its approach toward setting for the evening. There were more armed guards at the door which they opened for us readily. Once outside, we walked a short distance before getting into modified golf carts that were parked next to pickup trucks. Now outside, it was easier to see the surrounding area, which was meticulously well-kept, even in these times. The building we left had a modern look and plenty of windows. I was able now to see three more, smaller buildings, each no taller than three or four stories high. They were all evenly spaced with a large courtyard in the middle. There were manicured bushes and semi–mature trees dotted along the pathways which led to each building. The building we were headed to was the farthest away, westward of all the buildings which I now realized, save for the main building, made a loose triangle shape. We arrived at two large metal double doors and were quickly ushered inside. Again, there were more armed security guards waiting to escort us into the building. Each of them addressed my uncle and gave him a nod while only giving me a quick look– the kind meant only to confirm my identity in their minds. Once inside, I saw the interior was decorated in more comforting and soothing colors. I was probably wrong but the walls were a light taupe color with stripes of maroon in between. A professional interior designer might call it something more specific. As we walked further into the atrium or gathering area, there was a small fountain in the middle. Off to the side there was a desk with an attendant who was on the phone, most likely announcing our arrival.

"Upstairs is where your new room will be, which is just on the second floor. The first floor has another lab and their living quarters. Some of security lives here too–

though they reside in every building except the one you just came from, which is mostly administration. Here, they'll be able to monitor you closely and meet all of your needs," Uncle Lloyd spoke confidently.

"It's looks nice here." I said trying to be appreciative.

We went straight to the elevators and to the second floor. Once we made it down the hall to my room I saw a more spacious and comfortable environment than my previous room. There was a living room in an area that included a TV and a CD player off to the side of my bed. A small bookshelf with a few books and some small house-plants sat underneath a window. I also had a private bathroom with a tub and a shower. The sleeping area looked more normal except there was a machine that mon-itored blood pressure and pulse rate nearby. The room was painted a pastel yellow and felt like all but something from home but again, it was better than the last room. I noticed several guys from the security detail left once we were there. One of them rattled off on their radio about how the transport was completed. There were now just three men from the five we had before.

"So, how do you like it?" My uncle spoke up after a moment or two.

"It's nice, it's better than before." I answered while still looking around.

"That's great. They'll still need to run their tests but they're able to carry on from here as well as the last space. Please don't give them such a hard time– they are do-ing as I say under my recommendations using their experience, okay?" He advised me, kindly.

"Okay, but I need to know what's going on too. I want to know." I told him.

"Alright, fair enough. It's getting late and you need to get settled in." He said as he stepped toward me to give me another hug. "I'm so glad you're alive," he whispered as he gave me a squeeze and kissed the top of my head. He concluded with, "I'll see you again shortly," and walked out of the door along with everyone else who had come to make sure I arrived. As it closed, it locked automatically. "*So much for not feeling incarcerated*," I said to myself as I sat on the couch and looked at the TV which was not yet on. I looked for the remote which I found to be on the end table and turned it on. The first channel that was on was the news network which had nothing but pic-tures of destruction and gore from Jersey City and the Camden area. The newscast described the infection of hundreds of thousands within the viewing area along with hundreds of thousands of people dead and missing. I sat in shock as I discovered nearly a week had gone by since that morning I overslept and woke up to all out hell. It was now Wednesday evening and the reporters vowed to stay on air for as long as they could. They made claims that their building would be kept secure and they were on lockdown as well from the public. I watched repeated images of fires and more amateur video of people being attacked and killed. Before I knew it, the tears began to fall. The valium I'd been given a short while ago prevented a full outburst but from what my own feelings could manage it was still the greatest combination of both sorrow and shock.

After an hour or so the sun began to set and someone new arrived at my door.

There was a slight knock which at first I'd paid no attention to. By the second or third time though I yelled out, "I can't open it from in here." in my laziest tone. A few seconds later someone with a cardkey must've swiped it open because there was a clicking sound and the door was opened. At first glance I thought a teenager walked in with a food tray but as she walked over and sat down I noticed she was just a really young-looking adult. It could've been due to her straight black hair, tanned skin and heavy eyeliner. Her short height and tiny frame helped her youthful look as well. There was something about her that gave me comfort, though. She seemed a lot less authoritative as she said, "Hey there Seanna!" and sat down the tray, removing the cover that concealed a few slices of pepperoni pizza and a salad.

"Thank you, it looks good– I'm starved." I told her as I sniffled a little.

"Yeah I figured you might be a little hungry for something other than broth and bread," she laughed. "I'll be your nurse, most of the time from this point on, by the way. My name is Mia– it's nice to meet you."

"It's *interesting* to meet me I'd say. Did they tell you I'm . . . " I said, referring to my health status.

"Of course I know, silly– I have your chart right outside," she interrupted and chuckled again.

I kind of gave her an awkward look, though the way she said it was funny to me too. "I thought they were sending in a candy-striper or something because you look about fifteen," I replied.

"I've been told, though I'm not much younger than you."

"Yeah, well– it's nice to meet you too," I said. I meant it.

Mia waited for me patiently while I took a few bites from the salad and pizza where afterwards we also had a lengthy conversation. She asked me about my occupation and was pleasantly surprised that I too was in the health care field. Though it was just last week before everything happened– it seemed like it'd been a year since I worked as I recalled some of the experiences I had. I told her about my ambulance partner Ronny and how I hoped he was still alive and with his family now in Pittston. In my own mind I thought about how things might've gone for me had I took his advice and went with him in the first place. I found out from Mia that she's from Wisconsin originally and has one brother– that she hasn't heard from either. She also revealed that both of her parents are deceased already from an auto accident three years earlier. She moved to New Jersey for schooling and found a job working for a hospital nearby afterwards. Mia ended up at this research facility after being a paid research participant herself in a clinical trial in which she saw 'unique nursing opportunities' posted up on a job board. That was two years ago now.

I didn't know why they decided to send Mia in after Nurse Laura's excellent care and companionship, I joked to myself. Then I thought more about my earlier behavior and decided I would try to make amends for what happened with Dr. Chavan and his nurse. According to my uncle, I'm the niece of the top dog on campus so why not pull a few strings and prevent a reprimand or two?

"Does Dr. Chavan work or live in this building?" I asked Mia.

"He's here often– at least a couple times a day," she replied. She looked as if she wanted to know why, so I told her.

"I kind of want to apologize for what happened earlier. It wasn't his fault what I did and I'll talk to my uncle about it if I have to– if it means it'll keep him out of trouble," I said.

"I should be able to get a phone in here, especially if it's a call to one of the extensions here on site," she responded. I immediately thought about my parents and Graham but this time I said nothing.

I asked her if she could try right away and she stood up right away. She took my tray of half-eaten food and told me she'd return with the phone, if she could. A few minutes later, Mia came back with her own card key and a phone in hand. "I promised I would stay here with you while you make the call and bring the phone back as soon as we're finished," she said as she found a phone jack, plugged it into the wall and brought the cordless receiver to me. In her pocket she pulled out a piece of paper with a four digit extension written down. I took the phone from her, dialed the extension and got a brief recording. It was the doctor's voice with a general greeting and as I heard the beep I quickly blurted out, "Um, hello doctor, this is Seanna– I was just calling to apologize for earlier. I don't want you to get into any trouble or anything. I would like to say it to you personally so when you have time, I'm hoping you'll stop by." I ended hesitantly with a "Thanks," before I ended the call, hoping he'd understand I sincerely meant it. Mia collected the phone and left before I laid my head down on the arm of the couch and drifted off to sleep.

I dreamt for the first time since the days at my own place as my mind apparently became unfastened by all of the recent events that took their course. I dreamt I was back at my apartment in my living room but all of the contents were gone as if I had moved out, or hadn't yet moved in. I was disappointed everything was gone so I walked to my bathroom where it too was also empty of my possessions. I went to my bedroom next where I opened the door and instead walked into Graham's bedroom at his house. This time, parts of an event occurred from a year ago when I went to his place after I hadn't seen him in two weeks. He had just returned from a trip to Spain with Chad and Darin. Once he called to let me know he made it home, I drove over and went up to his room where he was still in the middle of unpacking. We were supposed to go out for dinner but needless to say, we didn't leave his room until much later in the evening. In my dream however, when we were in the middle of making love, I was on top and I told him, "*I'm going to get the virus. It's okay, you're safe.*" We both were enjoying ourselves in the moment but he replied, "*Ssshh, we all die.*" He put his hands on my hips so our movements could be in unison and after a minute and a few deep thrusts, we both exhaled in pleasure. I threw my head back in enjoyment but when I looked back at him, smiling and relieved– Graham was no longer Graham as I knew him. The same wild look in Darin eyes that I saw up close as he attacked me was now in Graham's eyes too. Instead of the warmth that I frequently enjoyed from him— he felt cool to the touch. In my dream I had no reaction to his physical change. Instead, I leaned over to his face, kissed his forehead and whispered, *"Love,"* as I got up and stood over him. He began to groan like a dead one. I said it like it was to be expected and was nearly at his bedroom door when he got up unclothed in an effort to stumble after me. I wasn't scared, however I too was stark naked and opened the door to his room and closed it shut again. I abruptly woke up on the couch with Mia at my side, her hand patting me gently in an attempt to wake me.

"It's time for your medications again Seanna, bare with me and I promise I'll be quick so you . . . "

"No it's okay, I'm up," I said a little startled as I sat up and readied my arm for the injections. Sensing the surprise, Mia asked me if I was feeling okay.

I told her I was fine, but she responded with a look of skepticism as she reached into her scrub pocket and pulled out a new digital thermometer and unwrapped it from its packaging. She took no protests from me as she went into 'nurse mode' and directed me to open my mouth in a tone that wouldn't tolerate any protest. We sat there motionless for the few seconds it took to beep, signaling a reading.

"One-hundred two-point five," Mia read out loud. She looked a little puzzled as she grabbed my chart from the table and flipped a few pages. I could sense she was hiding her concern from the hurried way she looked at the watch on her hand and reached for the syringes. I didn't know how to react because I felt like my temperature was on the rise. During the rest of the short time Mia was in the room she gave me the injections and said nothing to me except, "Okay, you should probably lie down with all this in your system now," as she grabbed the chart and quickly made her exit, minus all the pleasantries from earlier I'd gotten used to.

Feeling questionable, I followed Mia's advice but now became overwhelmingly nauseous, rushing to the bathroom, barely making it to heave the pizza and salad I indulged in a short time ago. I was surprised as I hovered over the white porcelain toilet— looking at the mostly undigested pieces of my dinner. I was shivering by the time I finished and hurried to clean myself up in hopes of preventing any further sickness. It felt comforting as I crawled underneath the cool sheets and exhaled in relief for completing the task. I laid there for no more than ten seconds before the swipe of the key card sounded from the outside. The door swung open, Dr. Chavan and Dr Strauss, stepped in, both of whom carried expressions of concern.

CHAPTER SEVEN

I don't know if those two figured I'd be walking on the walls but I figured in the short time between the walk from the bathroom and those precious seconds I spent laying facedown, horizontally on the cool sheets– I managed to feel some relief. Upon looking, I was pleased to see Dr. Chavan. I was hoping he was here because he'd heard my voicemail message and was ready to help me bury the hatchet, my self-inflicted hatchet.

"Well hello Doctor. Listen, I wanted to personally apologize for my behavior earlier," I began my short speech before I was cut off.

"Seanna, we need to get your temperature again," Dr. Strauss interrupted me as she gave me a quick visual inspection. I looked over to Dr. Chavan who was now at the other side of the bed setting up the portable monitor, adjusting straps and plugging it into an outlet nearby. She pulled out another digital thermometer from her lab coat pocket and barely waited for me to sit up before she had the metal end at my lips. Startled, I obliged her request and sat there in silence yet again waiting for the thermometer to signal its results.

"I did receive your message, by the way." Dr. Chavan quickly blurted without any eye contact.

"*Mmmhmm...*" I mumbled, keeping my mouth closed tight.

They moved at the same time when the thermometer beeped. Dr Chavan put a blood pressure cuff around my arm and the oxygen sensor on my finger. Dr. Strauss gently pulled the thermometer from under my tongue, glanced at the tiny screen and looked at Dr. Chavan who was also waiting.

"Same," Dr. Strauss said.

By now the monitor was up and running and their attentions were focused now on all it had to offer. I sat there for a few seconds before the continual silence between the three of us caused me to speak up.

"I do want to say, I apologize to both of you and probably everyone else I caused trouble for." I said as I looked at them both, though neither gave a hint they were paying attention to a word I was saying.

"I feel okay, though I just lost my dinner before you came in." I quickly added.

The machine blinked twice as the numbers finally stabilized. Dr. Strauss reached behind the bed where there were three boxes of assorted sizes of exam gloves. She put on a pair and told Dr. Chavan that she was going to set up a line and directed him to go get, 'the kit'. In the meantime she went to a drawer to retrieve the usual blood collection supplies; a tourniquet, butterfly needles along with similar, multi-colored test tubes from before.

"I see you're getting prepared," I said as I felt the anxiety rise.

There was still no answer from her as she worked at a quickened pace, having had all the tubes filled by the time Dr. Chavan returned. After gloving up, he began his part setting up the line, gently holding my right arm where the line was before. It was Dr. Strauss who left from the room this time. Using the same rubber tourniquet as before, Dr. Chavan found a vein and inserted the needle requesting that I stay absolutely still as he found a roll of paper tape to secure it in place.

"This will have to do until I can secure it." Dr. Chavan looked me in the eyes with growing concern. In that same moment, he leaned in closer taking a good look at them.

"Your irises, they look like blood is collecting around them." he said as he fiddled around in his shirt pocket to find a pen light and carefully inspected one eye at a time. I'd witnessed the same redness in the irises of the man who attacked me in the stairwell of my apartment but not in Darin's eyes. Maybe it was because I didn't have time or the guts to ask him to be still while I examined them for myself. I knew this was a bad sign, another of many that pointed to only one thing.

"Another symptom?" I said to him.

At that moment Dr. Strauss returned to the room. Dr. Chavan informed her specifically saying that it looked as if I had some intraocular inflammation and bleeding which she double checked for herself.

"I don't like the onset of these symptoms all at once," Dr. Strauss announced.

"Blood pressure is declining from earlier, ninety over sixty- three. Her temp is still at a low- grade fever and rising. Oxygen levels are decreasing into the mid-eighties." Dr. Chavan summarized everything they'd found in the last few minutes.

"I'm about to become one, aren't I?" I said as I swore under my breath.

They both stared at me.

"I feel fine, seriously. I mean, I'm talking to you still. I'm able to think, listen and reason. I'm not going to attack anyone either." I didn't mean for my voice to quiver when I said 'attack' but the fear was beginning to amplify itself again with this turn of events.

"I think it's time." Dr. Chavan said to Dr. Strauss, who appeared to be in working out something in her head.

"We're not even close to being ready yet," she responded in a low tone. There were just three of us in the room but I could sense her words were particular.

"Ready- for what?" I asked in between glances at the two of them.

"Give her another dose of the antibiotic and I'll go make some calls. She doesn't need to be up either." Dr. Strauss blurted in an even lower tone I could still hear. She left in a hurry without another word.

"I was hoping we'd have more time," he said under his breath, reaching into his lab pocket for the pre-filled syringes I was getting all too familiar with. Similar to the other times after the injections, I found myself becoming disconnected but this time I felt more afraid, which made me unable to relax completely. Unlike the feeling of floating away, my mind raced like a mouse in a maze coming to dead end after dead end in a frantic attempt to find a way out. My only exit would be safety and good health. I'd just been given proof that physiologically I was dying; the decline in my bodily functions said so. Plus, I saw with my own eyes everything from the undigested food I couldn't tolerate to the vials of blood they'd taken and were now testing, just like before. I knew these tests would show that organs such as my liver were declining in function just like the machine next to me that said my blood pressure and oxygen levels were also falling. Feeling pitiful about my situation, I lay back in the bed pulling the blanket up over my legs and rested on my side, as best I could with the line in my arm. Dr. Chavan saw the worry I had but there was no more conversation between us. He seemed distracted too and left me alone to my thoughts and the cruel reality.

I stared at the linoleum floor and the walls expecting to doze off rather quickly- because that's what had happened every other time I got a round of medications. I felt different this time. Being infected was one horrible thing however, my case was unusual enough to have a longer amount of time to experience the symptoms. I was convinced I'd meet the same end so in a way, none of it mattered. The destination was ultimate. Poor Ruthie and Darin had only hours to go through the transformation- if that's what one would call it. I was given a week. It made no difference because in the end we'd be the same.

It was now little before ten. I turned over to my left side, disregarding the discomfort, out of habit and closed my eyes wondering if the next time I woke up how much worse I'd be. Would they try to suppress the infection further with drugs or would I end up on a machine because I was the niece of the man in charge and they'd try a little harder to save me? Perhaps the friendly members in security would convince my uncle to look out for the group and end my life in order to keep everyone else safe? While I was running all the exit scenarios through my head, I heard a swipe from the card key outside on the door. I was too busy doing the self-pity thing to turn over and look to see who it was.

Instead I just spoke out over my shoulder, "I'm okay, just trying to rest a little."

There was silence for about three seconds as the only sounds were of footsteps coming into the room but when a voice spoke up I could feel myself nearly float off of the fabric I laid on.

"That's good to hear, cause even the dead don't rest these days."

I rolled over faster than one would expect, my self-included. There was my Graham, standing there next to Mia whom I could tell was utterly delighted with her surprise for me. I somewhat kicked the covers from around my legs and forgetting about side effects, rolled out of the bed and started towards him where he hurried to grab my arms to help support my unsteadiness and as far as the IV would let me go. I stopped just short of tearing the IV from my arm. He looked into my watering eyes. Acknowledging the boundaries of the infection, I gave him the longest hug anyone would imagine under the circumstances. He softly kissed my forehead and my cheek. I tensed a little, feeling scared for him, which he sensed. Feeling his arms around my waist and his strength was something like a payday of emotions I was long overdue for.

"It's okay, it's okay," he quickly whispered as his hands went in a slow circular motion, rubbing my back. I didn't want to let him go— ever again. It was like he already knew what was going on with my eyes because the next thing he did was look into them, studying them.

"It doesn't look too bad, does it?" I asked him as I looked down and away, a little embarrassed. It sounded like I was asking his opinion about a shirt I was trying on or an unexpected pimple or something.

"You can't really see it, unless someone gets close to you. Those browns are still beautiful, don't worry." he said reassuringly.

"I feel okay, but dude, I'm *scared*. It's not like what everyone else has. I should've been gone by now." I said. At that time I shifted my thoughts and attention to Mia who was still standing there silently.

"Thank you Mia for bringing him to me! Did you guys have to sneak up here or something?" I asked, stepping around Graham but holding on steady to him. The tears were delayed but they fell one by one causing me to wipe my eyes several times.

"You're welcome and don't worry about it. Of course he wanted to see you too, so much he was willing to climb up through the window— that can't be opened." Mia chuckled. "You two enjoy yourselves because we gotta be outta here before the night nurse comes in to check on you in a few minutes," she warned.

"Have you seen my parents? I was told they're here. Are they okay?" I turned towards him as he lifted my wrist to inspect the now sutured bite mark.

"I haven't yet," he replied.

NGT covered a lot of ground with its multiple buildings I could tell it was organized to where the employees were located only where they resided and worked. There weren't any people outside just strolling around, taking a walk. To be outside required some security, just in case.

"You know, that's weird because I've been to this building and to one other since we were brought here and there's no sight of them. No one has mentioned them being here by name. They're organized here beyond belief— like they were preparing for this all. They know you and I came in together along with every other couple or group that arrived here. They should know we all want to be reunited." Graham said of the staff here, referring to our relationship.

"Are they being good to you?" I asked.

"Yeah, especially after the tests confirmed I wasn't infected. I'm even pitching in with some of the agricultural stuff around here since they're concerned the food supplies will dry up eventually. Some of the roof tops are already being converted into greenhouses. They'll convert two of the floors in one building as well. I think the plan involves being here long term. You should see the stuff they are bringing in everyday from God knows where," he said.

That didn't bring me any comfort because I knew it wasn't solving the main problem.

Graham hugged me repeatedly as he told me he was starting to assume he'd never see me again. His ideas were similar to mine, that the staff here was likely trying to distract him at every inquiry about me. He also talked about the moment I was attacked in his living room— how the guys from NGT kicked in the back door at precisely the same time the dead man came through the front window. I then described to him the bouts of what I called pain attacks that felt like every muscle in my body was being wrung like a dishcloth, how it was only recently my eyes had developed the red ring around the irises and how the doctors were giving me antibiotics and tons of pain killers.

"I want to kiss you so bad," I told him when I looked into his eyes. I was serious as the sun but he just chuckled and did this smirk thing with his lips that he knows appeals to my primal senses.

"I know, me too." he responded.

Mia interrupted us and pardoned herself for having to end our little rendezvous. I made her promise that she'd bring him back to me as we held each other one last time, for now.

"I'll do what I can. Until then I'll look for a roster with everyone's name here and see if I can find out where your parents are. They've gotta be in one of these buildings," Mia said before going to the door, opening it and looking both ways to make sure they could leave unnoticed.

"I love you." Graham said as he kissed my forehead and went near the door to wait for Mia's indication it was okay to walk out. Within seconds they were both out of my room and Mia directed a quick wink and a smile at me. She pointed at him and gave me a thumbs up before she closed the door and they were both gone. Mia had made my day and I don't know how I would ever repay her for that moment of selflessness. I was infected and because of that I could've caused a lot of trouble if something went wrong while they were here with me. Mia had to see the good in this scenario and weigh it against the odds.

I quickly returned to my bed— overwhelmingly energized from seeing Graham. It was as if I could still feel his embrace and feel the vibration of his voice in my ear. Though I certainly didn't want to, if I changed into one of those things at least my last good memory for now, would be my time with him and knowing the love for each other that we had newly reaffirmed in our hearts and minds.

I felt sorrow in my heart as well, knowing that my parents were probably overwhelmed with concern for myself and Junior. I recalled my Uncle saying they would attempt to search for my brother once they felt it was safe enough. I missed my brother and needed him just as much as I needed to see my parents– because he was out there, maybe even alone by his self to fight off the dead that were killing and eating anything with life in it.

After some time– perhaps thirty minutes, I was able to calm down and drift into a state of rest. I felt only slightly conflicted, not because of the valium being ineffective but because of a strange impulse that wrestled in my mind and beneath my skin. It was both intense and oddly erotic in nature and attempted to correct itself from my dream before. It was another version from my memory of when I went to see Graham at his house after his trip from Spain. The same, repeated events took place but instead of Graham turning into a dead one, he laid there complacent as I bit a chunks of flesh from his body only seconds after we made love. He didn't scream as there was no indication of pain even. After the height of our session, there was this silence as I kissed his shoulder and smelled his skin. I put my arm over him as we laid in his bed and I spontaneously bit into his arm and bit again, chewing– though I couldn't recall what the taste of his flesh was, his blood spilled, into the sheets and onto me and I hovered back over onto to him and continued to take sections by the mouthful from his arms, chest and neck. I continued to bite until I hit bone, and sometimes not even bothering to chew, just swallowing and letting his tissue and skin satiate some unfamiliar desire. I knew in my conscious that this was bad, as I even bit into the part of his throat containing his vocal cords. He was left with only being able to nod his head when our eyes met– signifying he was okay with what I was doing. It was only then I realized I was terribly wrong– I was one of them, a dead one! I jumped off of his bloodied body and ran toward his bedroom door where I opened it and instead of my hallway like dreamt before, I was still in his house. Knowing this was different and perhaps even real this time I ran out of the room, naked as a bird but managing to wake up as I was rounding the banister to head downstairs.

I had awakened again from this dream and discovered it was two o'clock in the morning. I was in reality and I'd slept nearly three hours.

I gained mostly anxiety from the dream, or nightmare, it seemed. Was this a premonition? Sweat now poured from me even while I was experiencing chills. It felt like the aggregate pain in my shoulder and arm was only a heartbeat away from going into a full-body attack. From the bed I looked over my head to see if there was a phone device so I could call someone. It was like everything was on cue because my heart rate and pulse, instead of going upwards, fell quickly and I began to shake uncontrollably. I watched as the monitors responded by beeping loudly. I rolled to my back as the physiological processes took over. I was unable to yell, instead I could be thankful that soon after I saw a few unfamiliar faces hovering over me and shouting words I could see from their lips but could not hear. I saw one of them yelling and in a seemingly slower motion pointing in a repetitive motion, away from me.

CHAPTER EIGHT

Upon opening my eyes, my vision was quite blurred at first. The room I was now in had a much brighter light than before. I saw the shape of a person I couldn't identify as a man or a woman approach me and stick a needle in my arm. I knew for sure because I felt a pinch followed by the sting of the fluid as it entered my blood stream. My whole arm, shoulder and suddenly the rest of my body felt warmer as it circulated and reached every artery and vein. I was laying flat on a bed- restrained yet again; this time at the arms, chest and legs which I felt was secured very tightly, resisting the slightest movement. Within seconds I assumed whatever I was injected with travelled throughout my system because my eyesight cleared from its foggy presentation. Instinctively I blinked a few times and was able to see it was Dr. Strauss standing in front of me with a syringe in her hand, which she discarded immediately. I was now in a room I would guess was a part of the laboratory due to the partially tiled white walls and lack of all other essential comforts that surrounded me previously. The room had nothing else in it but the bed, me snugly secured to it and the doctor. Within seconds my eyes caught sight of a few others as they observed me behind the glass of a smaller room attached. One set of eyes belonged to my uncle Lloyd who put on a nervous smile when our eyes met.

"Seanna, can you hear me?" Dr. Strauss said in a commanding tone, which wasn't different from any other time I heard her speak. I turned my head, a little startled from her abrupt voice. I should've said something but my voice and mouth were slow to respond.

"If you understand me, nod your head or speak," she commanded again.

I turned my head again toward the group of people in the room with my uncle because one of them moved to write something down and it caught my eye. My uncle looked on, intent to follow my every movement too, just as everyone else was. I didn't notice him at the first glance but soon I saw Davenport was there in the tiny room as well, standing right next to my uncle. I'd guess they were about fifteen feet or so away from me but I could read every expression on his face as he stared at me. It looked as if he would kill me right this second if Dr. Strauss, or anyone for that matter, gave him the okay.

"Seanna, do you understand me?" Dr. Strauss said again loudly, looking more intently in my eyes. She was about to turn toward the group observing me– perhaps to give up but I startled her by trying to clear my throat. It could've been mistaken as a growl or a rumble because it startled the doctor and she turned to me, looking as if she didn't know what to expect.

"I understand you– you don't have to yell... You're always yelling," I said after clearing my throat a few times more.

"She's verbally responsive," she said to the relief of everyone else watching with her.

"Can you tell me how you are feeling?" She continued on.

"I've felt better." I said slowly, responding to her question everything seemed unfamiliar– my surroundings, my own body included.

"How is your vision? Can you see my hands?" Dr. Strauss continued as she held her hands out away from both herself and me.

"I can see," I said before the door to the smaller room opened and my uncle came into the room. Davenport followed right behind him. I was able to see the handgun in its holster on his right side. I attempted to clear my throat again because it seemed a little sore and was reminiscent to the time after I had surgery to remove my appendix when I was fourteen. It was on the verge of rupturing because I walked around for two days with a fever and abdominal side pains but didn't tell anyone until I could barely stand up straight to go to my next class at school. I woke up from the emergency surgery experiencing hardly any pain except the feeling similar to a dusty barbed wire being shoved down my throat. This was the same feeling I had now.

"Seanna, my dear niece, how are you?" My uncle interrupted the doctor as she was continuing her verbal examination. I could tell he was excited and once again genuinely pleased at my consciousness.

"What happened?" I asked. "I remember waking up, not feeling well– I tried to call for someone but I couldn't move," I recalled from memory. I also tried not to include my rendezvous with Graham courtesy of Mia when I quickly recounted the last hour I was last aware of.

"That was two nights ago. That was moment the virus took its course and you were found near death. We barely had the necessary resources to safely induce you into a coma but they were able to bring you back and maintain your life artificially until we could get a hold of the proper treatments," Lloyd informed me.

"Wow." was all I could respond with.

"It took five minutes of resuscitation efforts to bring you back but you are here, sure as I am speaking to you. You were kept alive by machines for the last two days– but you, you came back. Our experimental methods worked!" His voice rose with excitement.

I didn't feel the same way he sounded. I mean, he sounded as if everything was okay and I could go back home and laugh at all of this like it was on a movie or something. I didn't respond because in truth, I was extremely weak. I don't know if it was due to lack of nourishment or injury, or the fact that according to my uncle I was dead and brought back to life, avoiding the expectations of the virus and instead being sustained by machines for the last two days. In all likelihood it was probably all three.

While my uncle went on presumably talking about my miracle revival, I saw Dr. Strauss respectfully giving him a chance to go on with his showcase because that was what my uncle was all about; his own grandeur and flair. Bless his heart; I've always thought most times he wouldn't be able to tell the difference between a live audience or his own mirrored reflection- it was all the same to him. I took the few seconds and looked at my arms which besides the restraints were not covered. I saw the grey paleness that replaced my former healthier tone and it looked quite disturbing. It was as if my skin was in need of some serious sun- not to mention that since I'm half Black, I always looked sunkissed, even in the dead of winter. The scar on my left arm from the bite was not visible from the angle I was laying in but I was sure it was still there.

My Uncle must've wrapped up his speech because the room was silent and looked at me. I answered with a half-crooked, weak smile. He smiled back at me, approached me and patted my head several times. After simply saying an "I'll see you again short-ly," he walked back into the tiny room where I saw him shake a few hands and exit out of another doorway. Davenport stood there still in the room with Dr. Strauss and I where I put forth my best effort not to look at him. From what I saw briefly, he was noticeably freshly shaven and might even be considered attractive to someone who had not been shot, twice now via bullet and dart. He also looked younger and more rested now without the five o'clock scruff he wore the other times I'd seen him. I could tell that I was being inspected from head to toe by his guarded and doubtful glances. Davenport must've been bored and satisfied with my new accommodations because he stood there only a few seconds longer with his arms crossed, let out a sigh, and left the room also. Dr. Strauss was handed a clipboard while the door was open where she wrote down a few things and focused her attention to the questions from before.

"Are you feeling any anger or hostility right now, Seanna?" She walked over to me saying.

"Not particularly." I responded.

"My team and I are trying to assess your aggression levels, *particularly* the need for those restraints on you right now, so as much detail as you can give would be helpful to us and possibly beneficial to you," she went on.

"No, I don't feel any hostility or anger. I can speak, I *know* who I *am!*" I spoke up with all my strength.

Dr. Strauss stood motionless, almost as if she didn't believe a word I was saying.

"Really, I mean it. The last thing I remember was another one of those pain attacks coming on and I wanted to call for someone- but, I guess I didn't get to . . . I re-member someone trying to help, they stood over me . . . That was it, now I'm here." I said as I paused for a second to go over the moments mentally as I recalled them outloud. I was telling her the honest truth.

"I don't know if I am one of those things or not- you tell me, but I know I don't feel like killing or eating a human being okay?" I added, for the record.

"Hold still," Dr. Strauss said as she pulled out a penlight device from her pocket and examined my eyes, looking into each one- twice.

"There is only slight pupil restriction with the light and continued evidence of hemorrhaging around both the irises and corneas," She reported out loud before turning the light off and returning it to her pocket.

"You're thinking the other shoe hasn't dropped, aren't you?" I asked her as she stepped back and looked at my arms and the rest of my body.

She didn't answer but returned to the rest of the group in the tiny room, leaving me there awkward as ever on this bed that I figured had to be designed for the criminally insane. I laid there looking up at the lights wishing yet again to be in another place- anyplace other than this fish bowl circus that I was the main attraction of. After a few minutes and she hadn't returned, I thought about yelling out but then I thought about how it would look to them. It would look like I was being hostile or aggressive and thus would cause more speculation to my status of whether or not I would attack at the first opportunity. I also thought about begging and crying, letting them see a little emotion- which would be easy I think because- well, because I was in the perfect scenario to beg but then how would they expect me to act if they decided not to pay me any attention? I'd probably get aggressive and seem hostile. For now, I was faced with a dilemma I had no choice but to go along with being silent and submissive until another option presented itself.

I closed my eyes- still fatigued from everything that was going on. I kept them closed too because the bright light shining on me from the ceiling was annoying and with my head basically forced to look straight, I focused on taking breaths of air. That little dialogue was a blessing I realized, coming from where I'd been.

Dr. Strauss returned into the room with a man that I recall seeing from my first night here. I opened my eyes to look at them both, not knowing what to expect. I remembered being told that he was from administration. With his plain white shirt and slacks, sans the blazer, he flashed a quick smile when our eyes met. It was quite obvious now that I was the fascinating new science project. It would likely be in my best interests to accept that I would probably have a long line of visitors and gawkers who would be filing past the glass wall to get a look at the sole survivor infected from this virus. While Dr. Strauss briefed the man using some medical terms I was familiar with, my imaginative side surfaced as I thought about all the little things I could impress them with. Besides memory and intelligent conversation, I could show them I could still do math, read and perform my old job- same as before, if they'd give me someone to work with. I could dress up and groom myself in front of a mirror and they'd clap and sigh in awe, especially if I pointed at someone, batted my eyelashes and smiled.

I chuckled to myself before the doctor saw me and said, "What's so funny?"

She waited for me to say something but resumed her agenda after a few seconds of silence. She briefly went over her last conversation with me as chairs were brought in and the two sat and while Dr. Strauss began to gather information from me about the events of the day that brought me to the research facility, including how I initially became aware of the viral outbreak. They asked me background questions, which I was sure they knew the answer to but had to be stated by me, for the record. They asked me a few general questions about my upbringing as well as my current living situation and occupation. Part of me knew that they were testing me as well as gathering information— noting any delays in my responses and mood changes during the questioning. I tried to stay at an even emotional level with my responses. What was difficult for me was to stay involved in the conversation because it seemed my concentration was hard to maintain. I wouldn't ordinarily be described as a chatterbox anyways— I was used to being observant, but after a number of questions my mind fluttered back and forth from past events. I kept going back to the moment the dead man's teeth went into my arm. Every few seconds I'd get a refreshed imaged, only in more detail, about the very instant when his teeth made contact with my skin and tissue. After a few times I could recall his yellowish-grey, clouded eyes, and the blood stained suit he had on. I could remember his receding hairline and the open, unhealed gash on his face. I recalled his filthy fingernails and hands which had cuts on them but were covered by dirt and small shards of glass from the window he had just fallen through and crawled over in order to get to me. None of those details however, were as disturbing as his odor as it was again similar to the smell of fresh clay and rotted meat.

"Can you tell me what's going on with me, now?" I asked, while fighting back shivers.

Dr. Strauss wore reading glasses but she took them off and blinked her eyes several times while looking up at the ceiling, in my opinion, to gather her terms together so maybe I would comprehend.

"Seanna, you may not understand everything that's going on with you because, well, we don't either. We're in the process of figuring it out," she started.

"I know I should be one of the dead by now." I replied wearily.

"You're correct. My job is to figure out why you aren't." she said.

"I was told the same thing earlier. I want to know how I get to be the exception to a pretty clear rule." I said.

"Science is and always has been slow and steady in its progression. Sometimes it takes months of round the clock work in order to bring minute amounts of significant data— which then requires repeated tests to ensure validity. Our lab is looking into the genetic aspects to identify the structure of this virus. Part of our task lies with finding a vaccine since finding a cure is highly unlikely with the amount of damage and decomposition that rapidly takes place in the average infected person. That damage is irreversible unfortunately. You know from your ties to healthcare that most often the answer is in prevention— in this case our goal is to protect healthy cells and whole bodies from invasion." she spoke in a monotone fashion

"I understand. What about my scenario: 'Girl gets infected but lives to tell about it?'" I questioned. I managed to spark a reaction from the doctor's associate.

"That's where things get interesting Seanna. You could look at the Earth and pin-point a hundred labs that are working feverishly to map this thing genetically from beginning to end to find the solution. They all have nothing but samples from dead specimens and live zombies to collect from. Not us though, we're working with a live survivor, confirmed infected: you and that puts us ahead of the game. The CDC and WHO can't even come close." The man said, speaking up with his sales pitch and opinion of the scenario. I looked for his ID badge because everyone around here had one. His was missing.

"I have something everyone else is missing– that's why I'm still alive?" I said.

Strauss spoke up again, "Your symptoms are worsening but I have my theories. We're trained scientists first. The lab is where we'll find our answers. Our hope is that we find them long before we run out of resources for you. Those medications you've been given are quite necessary to prevent further decreases in functioning, which may lead to death or otherwise, we just don't know at this point. Everything is new. Every perspective explored from this point has never been challenged or documented therefore there is no official treatment."

"I'm on thin ice, got it." I replied.

The rest of the conversation was brief. A few more doom and gloom hypotheses regarding my reaction to their new treatment plan and they were hesitant to go along with it. I was informed I was only person so far to have 'survived' for this long, which was going on nine days– including the resuscitation efforts that took place two days ago. I was told by the man in the room the treatment could eventually kill me as well but in any event, my full cooperation was necessary and appreciated. Darn, there was to be no more episodes of me wanting to leave, specifically in the form of myself getting up and heading for the front door. Both of them waited on my verbal agreement to that. In return, I had both the doctor's and her male assistant's agreement they would do everything they could to keep me comfortable and as less confined as possible, provided that my symptoms and behavior patterns remained the same.

It didn't take long for me to realize there was a whole lot of grey area in their promises but they were right, I had nowhere better to go. Not putting too much on the medicine's reliability for the long term, at least for now I could agree with the plan. Right now, I didn't feel great but here at least I was still alive. I told them I wanted to be kept informed about my own progress, good or bad– so that I could come to terms with everything if things took a turn for the worse. It was shocking to discuss the very real possibility of the end of my life at such a young age. I suppose in the last week, thousands of those afflicted like me had no opportunity to be so thorough and take their time with such discussion. Some probably died in a few hours or maybe even within a day but I bet the time was spent in a sorrowful panic with lots of crying and pleading for life before they slipped into their comas and eventually died, after which, there was another problem.

As the two got up from their chairs Dr. Strauss looked at her associate and said, "Should we do it?" He replied, "I think it'll be okay, right Seanna?" I looked at them both nervously and smiled as they both went to unfasten the restraints. I was so happy after I slowly got up to recover my balance, I quickly hugged the doctor. She definitely didn't expect this from me. She probably didn't appreciate the spontaneity but I wasn't about to worry about it. I was extremely weak, tired and my whole body felt like it wasn't mine. I quickly assured them that I was okay; slow at first with walking but that I could manage. She used her keycard and thumbprint on a reader to let us out of the room. I wasn't able to see from inside the room but immediately by the doors, there were two guards who followed behind us as we went to exit this area. We walked past a few glass walled rooms with several people in lab coats working with various machines and the occasional microscope. This time I felt protected instead of being escorted, though I was sure they were watching me closely.

There was a hallway we passed on our left side that was seemingly more solitary and had about half of the amount of lighting as the rest of the area. They appeared not to have any windows whatsoever. There were three or four doors on one side only down that hallway. One of the doors vibrated and a slight moan came from the other side. I shivered and could feel the hair rise on the back of my neck almost instantly at the sound. Dr. Strauss heard it and hesitated in her stride.

"What's down that hallway back there?" I asked as we walked few more yards and took a right where there was a short entryway with two sets of security doors.

"Specimens to take samples from," she replied as she used her thumbprint and keycard to unlock the first set of automatic doors which were all metal, and quite heavy to manually open.

The second and last set of doors was even more secure as it required you to be buzzed out by someone who was watching from two video cameras and could hit the switch to allow the doors to be opened. Past the secured doors was a small foyer area with an oversized elevator. Once again there was a card scanner which allowed the elevators to be called and again it had to be used in order to select a floor once you were inside. I was familiar with that system from the hospital because they only wanted visitors and patients in certain areas and they had to be accompanied by staff otherwise. We had to be on the lowest basement floor 'B2' because there was an additional 'B1' followed by the first and second floors. It didn't take long before the doors opened and I could see sunlight– presumably early morning sun.

We slowly but purposefully walked back to the same room I was in the last time. Outside of the room by the doorway there was a small cart that contained blood draw supplies. On the top shelf there were collection tubes, tourniquets, and an assortment of different sizes of butterfly needles, gauze and tape. On the next shelf was the more serious stuff such as IV bags and saline solution. I was already well acquainted with all of these things from my line of work. Seeing it all neatly sectioned off into their own organized bins caused me to remember how I was playfully teased for being so particular about the setup of the supplies in the ambulance I had for the shift. Though some neglected to restock the ambulance at the end of their day like they were required to, I had a "my bus, my rules" approach that made things easier for me even though it slightly irritated my supervisor Barb.

Once I got settled in again, I decided I wanted a long, hot shower. Without any objection from the request, I was given a fresh change of clothes by Mia who I was excited to see back on duty. I was enthusiastic in my, "Hey there, stranger!" to her but found it weird all she could muster was an expressionless and monotone, "Hello, Seanna." She quickly went out of the room and returned a few seconds later with her clipboard of paperwork and oddly enough an *In Style* magazine attached as she walked past me. I shook my head figuring that her reaction probably had less to do with me than the whole end of humanity scenario in general so I went on my way with turning on the shower water and getting out of my clothes. After all, the world as we knew it was falling apart and everyday more and more bodies joined the category of 'undead'. There were so many people I was worried about, my eyes watered at the thought of them. Mia said to me with a similar tone that she thought it'd be a good idea to leave the door to the bathroom open while she sat in the living area in case I needed her for anything. Again I noticed the lack of enthusiasm from her. In fact, she avoided any eye contact. I figured in the short time since I met her previously, we may not have worked our way up to BFF status but she gave out a much better vibe than what I was getting from her today. I felt she should've been able to express to me whatever was bothering her. I liked Mia and thought we got along fairly well. Maybe they told her to not get so attached to me because it was likely I wouldn't survive and she should distance herself and prepare for when that time comes. It sounded reasonable to me. It was the truth.

One thing I wasn't prepared for at all was my reflection in the mirror. This was the first time I could see my face in all its paleness. I did a doubletake, blinking several times and leaning in closer for inspection. In all honesty, I looked like a victim of a drowning with the exception of the blood in my eyes. I could recognize myself but it was nothing to be proud of. The scariest thing of all to me was that my reflection reminded me of a call we were dispatched to a few years ago during the Fourth of July holiday. Ronny and I were working mid-shift and considered ourselves lucky because we'd managed to have only four calls that day. One was a rear-end car accident which everyone refused treatment because there were only some minor cuts and scratches so we checked them out and informed them about our release of liability. The second call was for a middle aged woman who was experiencing chest pains and the third was for a teenager who was skateboarding near downtown and decided to try his luck on a stairwell despite the signs prohibiting it. Both got a ride to Lehigh at Cedar Crest but it wouldn't be hard to guess which one had a broken ankle and still managed to get a ticket from the police. Ronny and I were just short of a high five for the relatively uneventful shift when dispatch called about a possible drowning and rescue efforts for three boaters whose canoe capsized in Lehigh River. According to reports from dispatch they were out of the boat and in the water for more than twenty minutes. They found two of the boaters alive, slightly downstream but the last person was still missing. We were told to hang out at the initial location of the capsizing because the officers in charge of the rescue, judging from the river depth and flow figured the person would not be much father downstream given the timeline of events. We waited as the description of the last victim became more and more complete. It first started out as a young female and grew to a nineteen year old woman with curly brunette hair, dark tank top and jean shorts. The young woman's name was Charlotte; all of this was heard over the back and forth chatter of the radio from the police as our radios were on the same channel. Ronny and I waited nervously with the stretcher, defibrillator, warming blankets and oxygen ready for the next hour as hope faded for preserving Charlotte's life. If there was any part available in a miracle, we were all ready to join in. Unfortunately her time ran out because minutes later, she was found floating near a partially submerged tree less than two hundred feet from where they pulled her two companions out alive. We all still followed protocol– putting her on the stretcher, giving her oxygen and checking for vital signs. It was clear that she was no longer with us as I used my stethoscope to check for the slightest pulse. Her relatives were nearby and we wanted to be sure that every effort had been made to try to save her life. It was still considered a rescue effort and not yet a recovery but her cold, graying skin coming out of the cool water was the most obvious indication.

It was the same type of skin I saw in the mirror.

With all of my previous wounds feeling more numb today than ever before, I carefully removed the bandage from my shoulder, revealing a few sutures and some bruising around the area that was about the size of the bottom of a pop can. I was attempting to look at my shoulder backside in the mirror and with my dull skin I noticed it looked like the wound belonged to a body on an exam table at the coroner's office. I stepped into the shower and let the water freely run over the wounds. I spent at least twenty or thirty minutes washing my hair, body and just standing there thinking, breathing in the hot steam and hoping it would wash away all the soreness and hurt that overwhelmed me.

By the time I was done grooming in the bathroom, I had only my wet hair to deal with and after a bit of thought, I had decided I would probe a little in order to find out what was going on with Mia. Once I figured from every angle it couldn't possibly be me she was upset with, the least I could do for her was lend an ear. After what she'd done for me I owed it to her because I considered her a friend, if nothing else she was a nice person.

When she saw I was finished in the bathroom she promptly stood up.

"I was told that I should order you something light for breakfast. The doctors will be in soon to draw another round of blood from you. I should warn you, they may need urine from you as well." she said.

"I'm not too hungry. Is something wrong Mia? I mean, I know there's a lot going on." I replied, slipping in the last thing suddenly.

"I'll bring you some ginger ale and toast otherwise they will end up putting you on IV nourishment." she spoke, avoiding my question.

"I'll take the toast..." I began to say but was cut off.

"In the meantime, why don't you sit down and try to take your mind off of things. I brought you a magazine. It's one of my favorites. There's some cute summer dresses toward the middle section," she spoke as if it were more than a suggestion.

"Can't wait to take a look." I said, sounding confused as she strolled past me saying she'd come back with the soda and toast as soon as it was ready.

I thought I'd take some time to comb my hair before I tried to get comfortable. The shower helped somewhat as they upgraded my soap since the last time. Before I had some bargain brand that was unscented but this time I could tell it was one of my favorites, *Caress* in its original scent. I was satisfied before as the soap did its job but the simplicity of a particular smell that I was used to did wonders for my mood. The only vexing thing other than the condition I was dealing with was Mia's strange mood at the moment. I felt a little dizzy thinking I could move around at my normal pace so I moved slowly and sat on the edge of the bed with my comb in hand and started detangling. I had a selfish moment as the only thing I needed now was my professional strength leave in conditioner.

Once that task was finished, I walked over to the window to take a look outside. It was still sunny as the late spring warmth made its presence known in the growth of the new leaves and wild bushes nearby. Nearly everything was green and it was beginning to look as if the warmth was here to stay- just as it did with the dead.

I walked past the coffee table with the magazine on it from Mia's suggestion and picked it up to bring to the bed. Again, I couldn't understand what had Mia so distracted. Perhaps she'd found out where her brother was. Of course she could easily tell me that was what happened. Then again, it could be the condition her brother is in, if they did manage to locate him, if it were bad, I'd be in the same mood if it were my brother. No one else seemed to be in such a down mood so I figure things were still okay here at the research facility. As I slowly lay down and pulled the covers over my legs I felt a slight burning pain in my forearm again and then in my shoulder. It was no surprise there because I was simply trying to get comfortable. Eventually, I was able to lay on my right side and thumb through the magazine. I didn't read any articles in particular because my mind was too scattered to focus. Instead, I just thumbed through the pages looking at the different ads and style tips, wondering if they were still valid now and if perhaps they would adjust the color expectations to look appropriate on deceased persons now that they were up and about. It was difficult to see articles that were printed only a short time ago when everything was arguably okay- in a sense that all of the conflict and issues we thought of were now infinitesimal compared to the one problem we were dealing with now. As it miserably appeared now, who would be left alive and be able to solve this problem? If the internet were available by now, I'm sure there would be website hosting a growing list of all notable figures that were now amongst the not-so-dearly departed list.

In the magazine there were plenty of familiar celebrity faces in outfits and on the side an, "Own This Look For Less" statement with a similar styling suggestion. Finally, I got to the section called, "Summer Hotness" where it described the trend for the up-coming warm season. There was nothing spectacular about the first page for the article except they were expecting this season to be a colorful one, fashion wise. There were quite a few frilly summer one-piece dresses and a few multipiece layering tops but nothing super special. I saw a nice dress with an interesting bohemian pattern I would've probably purchased at the local mall in Allentown, if things would ever return to normal. It wasn't until I was three pages into the article that I saw something that was meant for me. It was a tiny note inconspicuously written off to the side in blue pen:

Your parents are here. They arrived before you. I cannot find them. There's a reason you've survived. Chavan knows why. Your room is probably being videotaped. Don't freak out. Finish the magazine.

Of course, she should've known I couldn't possibly follow those directions. I imagine if there was an actual camera in the room, depending on its angle, it would've caught me in a blank stare for almost a full minute. I was no longer casually paging through the magazine or skimming through the titles and short stories nor squinting to view the prices of the glitzy and beautiful clothing located in captions off to the sides. In fact, it was one particular caption off to the side, the one handwritten by Mia that just put me on notice about several very important findings. I sat there for a moment choosing to look over at the window which presented more cloudier and gray skies now. I thought it would buy me time to try and compose myself as those few sentences suggested a great number of faults within the organization called NGT– headed by my uncle that with good proof and reasoning, I thought was secure.

CHAPTER NINE

The door couldn't have opened at a worse time. The swipe of the badge heard from the outside gave me about a half of a second's notice which snapped me out of my contemplative daze. The thought of my parents not being kept here safe, put me right back at the state I was in before I left my apartment. With Graham nearby but still out of reach– yes, it was almost the same scenario as before– minus Ronny who'd keep a cool head for the both of us. I closed the magazine quickly, perked up, straightened my sad face and readied myself for whoever it was entering. It was another person, a nurse I assumed. She had a few syringes in her hand. She took a quick look at me and held the door open as Dr. Strauss followed behind her.

"Seanna my name is Louise, I'm here to help Dr. Strauss with your blood draw and medications," the middle aged woman spoke.

"Where's Mia?" I asked. I couldn't sound more concerned. I rose out of the bed quickly

"You should be in bed," Louise advised. "Mia is taking a little break. Apparently she's not feeling well. I imagine she'll come back when she's better," Louise added as she ushered me back to the bed.

Dr. Strauss put on some exam gloves from the cart outside and grabbed a few more tubes as both her and Louise laid out all of their supplies on the bed next to my legs. Louise tied a rubber band like string around my upper arm as she readied my arm for the draw. Noting its paleness she questioned the doc about the ease of getting a vein. Dr. Strauss must've been irritated as she shooed Louise away, saying she'd do it herself. Neither of them said a word to me but Louise stood close by with her gloves on ready to assist the doctor, if needed. The silence was killing me as she quickly worked to find the vein and get the tubes filled. I noticed there were three syringes filled with fluids.

"So what are you giving me now?" I asked her nervously.

"These are the same as before when you were downstairs. There are some medications to manage the pain– others are to hopefully help stop any further cell damage. We will run these new samples in the lab to see if we need to modify the drugs. They worked before; hopefully we'll have the same if not better outcome."

"These are experimental?" I asked.

"A few of them– yes, they have just been created by our group here– they don't even have a name. Remember what we talked about," She said, reminding me about the whole situation. There would be no clinical trials or FDA approval in an effort to be ethically sound about introducing new medications. I was all there was for a test population as the FDA was probably history as far as we knew anyways. Dr. Strauss finished up with the collection. I knew to hold the gauze over the puncture mark until the bleeding subsided. It didn't take long to clot. I was thinking the dead don't usually heal enough and the blood might've kept coming out if the skin didn't close itself, but then again I was not used to forensic side of patient care. There was no telling what this disease might have me or my body doing.

Dr. Strauss started giving me the injections, trying her best to get a vein for each of the three needles. I wondered if she was in on the lie that my parents were here as well. She seemed to be the type who could care less about my personal situation. It seemed she was instead, fiercely loyal to her job. Maybe that's why she chose to work in a lab versus with actual patients– who knows? All I knew for certain was that her bedside manner stunk and it seemed like technology probably was her best and only friend. She had no rings on her finger and the only bit of jewelry she wore was a pair of simple, small silver earrings.

Dr. Strauss hurried off with her metaphorical gold mine– those blood filled tubes. There was no telling what they'd find under the microscope once they took a look at it this time. Louise hung around for a few moments, noting things on the clipboard. She asked me how I was feeling which I responded I was the same as before. Truthfully, I was feeling so many things right now; confusion, anger about pretty much everything, worry, and a little bit of pain would've been a little more honest of a response. The door opened again as Mia walked in with a food tray. I was surprised to see her as she walked over to the bed and sat the tray on the nightstand. She acknowledged Louise and told her it was okay to leave– that she could manage from now on. Louise became a little resistant.

"I was told before we came up here that I was to stay with Seanna after her meds were administered in case she has another reaction." Louise said sternly.

"I think I am competent enough to handle that. Besides, they only called you to fill in because I wasn't feeling well earlier. I'm fine now so you can go take it up with Tom, Dr. Strauss or whoever," Mia said as she waved her hand with a little flare. It was just enough to send Louise on her way as she mumbled something under her breath. After the door shut I looked at Mia waiting on her cue for our discussion. I was never good at talking in code so I wasn't about to try to initiate anything. I admit though, after a few short seconds I was ready to burst because I wanted to hear the words from her mouth that my mom and dad were nowhere to be found and that my uncle was indeed lying when he said he was going to reassure them about my health status.

Mia looked at me and gave me a smile meant for the pitiful.

"You look tired."

"I'm not. I'm worried." I responded.

"There's your toast, ginger ale and apple juice. I will keep some water nearby because you need plenty of fluids,–" Mia began to inform me before I cut her off.

"I saw those dresses you were talking about. Are you sure they're your favorites? There may be some other ones in another catalog or magazine." I told her. I was hoping she understood me because that was the best I could do as far as talking in code.

"No, I'm positive. I haven't seen anything better, anywhere else. I checked several other magazines and nothing came close. All of the stuffs I saw were just ugly; they looked like they wouldn't fit right or be very comfortable. I know for sure when something looks decent. You can call me a *fashionista*. Here, let me help you get comfortable." Mia said as I took a few sips and bit the toast. It was cold and dry by now but I needed the nourishment. She fluffed a few pillows and pulled the covers up over me and walked around the bed to get my chart. She must've noticed my pulse hadn't been taken in a while so she went about taking a reading. From our ambiguous conversation I gathered that she said she was sure that my parents were not anywhere as far as residing in the facilities, she hadn't saw them anywhere either. I was so disappointed to find this out from her even though she told me earlier by writing it down. Telling me in code and hearing it from her mouth made it worse. Why would my uncle tell a lie like that?

"Are you sure?" I whispered as she rested her first two fingers on my wrist to get a pulse. She nodded her head slightly. There was complete silence as she wrote the numbers down on the chart and stood up.

"Try and get some rest. I'll bring you some more stuff to read, in a little while," Mia said as she glanced at the clock on the wall.

"By the way, try not to get too rattled but someone will be in here to check on you at least twice an hour. Most of the time it will be me," she added.

"I can't promise anything, anymore," I responded, feeling lower than ever.

Mia left me as usual and I managed to take my own pulse several times because I couldn't believe the results I was getting. Mind you, I didn't have a stopwatch but nevertheless I was quite used to taking a person's pulse. I would call myself experienced. According to that same experience, I was now getting a pulse reading of about twelve beats per minute. I felt like I almost died right then as I laid there and did the calculations in my head. I had to tell myself not to panic, that I hadn't died yet or at least remained dead according to what my uncle told me. This was the best place for me to be despite my unanswered questions and the elusive whereabouts of my family. For a short while I was probably okay– that was until I woke up to hell without the heat.

Someone was definitely going to have to fill me in because my next moment of awareness I found myself on the floor away from the bed, being physically restrained. Dr Chavan was there along with Mia, Louise and two other young men who were obviously petrified. Mia appeared to barely contain her fear. They were now wearing what looked to be protective clothing in the form of jumpsuits. In short, it looked like they were made from the same material as the bulletproof vests law enforcement wore however theirs were complete with sleeves and they also wore gloves made out of the same material.

"Seanna, can you hear me?" Mia stuttered but spoke quickly. Both she and Louise were stronger than they looked because I was completely pinned down while the two petrified men had most of their weight on each of my legs, restricting any movement as well. Dr Chavan was the only one standing up. He had two used needles in one hand and the other hand was outstretched signaling two armed men to stay where they were.

"I can hear you. What's going on? Why am I pinned to the floor like I just tried to–" I said as I started answering my own questions. The sad thing was, no one moved from over my arms and legs. Instead, there was just an odd few seconds of silence before Dr. Chavan said, "I think she's alright now." It was Mia who released one of my arms first as I slowly moved to encourage what little blood flow I had. I had to tell everyone else I was okay before anyone else moved. After a few seconds and a few more skeptical looks I was once again free. Louise was kind enough to help me stand up on my feet before she nearly ran out of the room. I heard Dr. Chavan quietly tell Mia, "You shouldn't put yourself in danger like that, next time wait for me." before he saw I was listening and he stopped speaking.

Apparently I just gave a new explanation to the term *nightmare*.

"What just happened?" I asked them again as I steadied myself to get over to Mia and the doctor. The two armed men stood attentively waiting by the door and were alert to my every movement.

"Tell her." Mia said to the doctor.

"They came back to check on you and you were . . . not yourself. It was a repeat incident of what happened downstairs earlier." he spoke quietly.

The doctor turned around and instructed the armed guards back to their original duties but had to reassure them that he would report the incident to Davenport himself right away once he was finished here because everything was normal now. He also took the opportunity to escort me to the couch where he performed a quick check of my vitals. Mia picked up on the routine and stepped out of the room, only to return seconds later without the jumpsuit, instead with gloves and more blood collection supplies. I sat there bewildered and admittedly dumbfounded at the calm and pro-fessional demeanor of the two working together, Mia patiently being attentive to the doctor as he filled the tubes and bandaged my now slightly bruised arm at the site where the blood collection had become common.

"We should put another line in, you think?" Mia said assessing my arm as she put a small piece of gauze and a strip of tape over the needle mark. Looking at my pale arm did not make things better and made me want to consider long sleeve shirts and pants from here on out– if I lived. There was a lot that could've been said right now but at this point it was unnecessary. They were probably thinking I was putting two and two together on my own– which they'd be correct. The conclusion I'd drawn about what happened to me a few minutes ago, although truthful and right on the money, was not a pretty one.

In short I started with, "I became one of them, didn't I?" Dr. Chavan stood still but eventually nodded his head as Mia looked away, seemingly almost ashamed of what happened. She spoke up and recounted the moments after which she came into the room to check on me and found me in the bathroom. The light was on and the door was open but when she came into the tiny space to check on me, I was standing there but unresponsive. Mia's voice got scratchy as she described my listless gaze and when after she called my name I walked toward her as she continued to step back. I said nothing during the whole incident. Mia reaffirmed several times that it seemed like I was not trying to attack her but that my behavior was more of a curiosity I may have had because I didn't recognize her. She said she then yelled for help, ran to the door and called the doctor on one of the nearby phones.

What happened next must've been what I overheard Dr. Chavan referring to, warning Mia about staying out of harm's way. From his obvious disapproval, Mia ran to tell Louise who was at a desk close by about what was happening and though Louise was reluctant, they both put on the protective jumpsuits and returned to my room before most of the people I remember seeing, could get here. It was a few minutes before the doctor along with two guys from the lab arrived with security and they were able to pin me down while the doctor gave me the injections.

Listening to Mia talk, I didn't know exactly how I felt because it seemed like she was describing another person's actions– someone who was definitely *not* me. This person was almost like a dead one, one of the same kinds of things that tried to attack me and on the second occasion was successful in infecting me. The whole lack of cognition and lethargic behavior was something I'd witnessed myself when the dead ones had no target to attack. It was when there was a potential victim that were able spring into action and though Mia tried to smooth it over by repeating how unaggressive I was, it was clear that the virus had taken over. I couldn't remember anything she was describing– I tried my best to recall any little thing she was describing but my last memory before waking up on the floor was when I was falling asleep. There was a few seconds of silence and Dr. Chavan was about to say something before I interrupted him.

"I know this means nothing next to the fear that you experienced but I'm sorry. I would never mean to harm you or anyone. I don't even remember anything you're talking about right now," I tried to explain to them.

"It's not up to the person, what they choose to do, after they come into contact with the virus," Dr. Chavan said reassuringly. "I'm afraid my colleagues aren't going to take any more risks now that this incident has occurred. I'll have to run this latest sample against the others and see what changes we can make, maybe we can increase the potency. It was less than two hours since the previous dose." he said. I could almost see his mind working at a feverish pace to come up with a solution. I slumped a little in couch, trying not to get too emotional. To add insult to injury I didn't have any tears to cry. It seemed I physiologically could not come up with the fluids necessary to create tears.

"Maybe I wasn't meant to survive this. You all know, I can't put all these people here at risk like this anymore. That same mentality is why it's out of control now– people are too busy trying to save the helpless. I mean, do we even know where this virus came from?" I asked as I looked to them both for an answer. I was finally coming to terms with the fact that I was a lost cause. The valuable tool I was told I could possibly be is turning out to be nothing more than an anomaly that would meet the same end like everyone else who crossed paths with it– whatever *it* was. I was beginning to accept my fate and though I didn't like it one bit I was convinced there was a bullet somewhere nearby with my name etched on it and waiting to be chambered. It would probably be Davenport and his side arm that would end it for me. He seemed more than willing to do the task the last few times we've met. Maybe the guy was a psychic before all of this happened and he is just acting on intuition and I'm the one who needs to accept the reality.

"Where will they take me?" I asked the doctor.

"They may or may not put you with the others." he said. I gave him a terrified look before he corrected himself.

"You'll just be in the same area. They won't put you in the same room of course." he said looking at Mia.

"Your uncle won't let them do that, there's no way!" Mia said in protest.

"Well I'd rather let them shoot me before I become a zombie guinea pig, there's no way I'm going that route." I told them. I meant it.

I shook my head in agreement with my own words. I wasn't going to harm either of them but I would get out of that place and take my chances with the outside world before I let them lock me up in one of those rooms I saw when we were leaving the lab area. I remembered the moans and how the hair on the back of my neck stood up as my ears picked up the auditory vibrations from deep sounds they made. They thought a cure was in my bloodstream and now it seems less likely, they are probably going to cast me in the room with the others like trash. Not if there's anything I can do about it.

The note Mia wrote in the article came to mind after which I asked Dr. Chavan what he knew about my surviving for this long. Since it appeared I was on my last leg, talking in code seemed pointless to me. He sighed at Mia, which she shrugged her shoulders and said she would go see if anyone was coming and try to hold them off as long as she could. The doctor and I were now alone and he sat in the chair next to next to the couch I was on.

"She wasn't supposed to say anything to you– yet." he started.

"You two– you're together aren't you?" I said.

He looked at me, a little startled by my statement.

"You might want to try a little harder if you want to keep it a secret. You guys are cute together though," I told him as I buried my face in my hands. If it weren't for the strong potential of the end of humanity, I'd say they had a chance.

"Mia thinks the room is bugged," I said, warning him to be careful of anything he tells me. I didn't care anymore about my feelings and personal business being recorded but I didn't want him to be forced to disclose his. After all, he still had a job to do.

"I'm sure they haven't. They wouldn't have had the time or the resources." he assured me.

"She says you know why I've made it this long– tell me." I said, looking at him for any sign of a reaction. It was easy to see this information was something that he was-n't entirely prepared to divulge because he took a few seconds and a deep breath before he spoke.

"I don't have all the answers and our machinery isn't the newest when it comes to mapping the genetic markers of the disease itself. We are doing a lot of stuff using gel electrophoresis which is like stone age since the mass spectrometer stopped working," he began to babble. He saw that I was lost and mumbled under his breath, "It's been awhile since your last Biology course, I assume."

"It's been awhile," I responded frankly.

"Well we can't be sure until we run it again but we've found a few commonalities between the markers of the viral DNA from other infectious hosts and the samples taken from you," he said while looking to see that I understand.

"Yeah but I've read we also have a lot in common with chimpanzees and even mushrooms," I said.

"Yes you're correct about the species of man. But for this virus I am saying speci-fically you– your remaining healthy cells. " he said. His rebuttal was frightening.

"Our research has been a lot like a crime show in regards to taking and compar-ing samples from the infected. Only a few of us know this but the only thing the virus and the samples from other infected individuals has in common seems to be you," he paused. "One of the reasons why we've been taking blood samples for you every few hours so we can track its progress. We can use a scale from zero to one hundred for any given sample as far as percent saturation of the viral content."

"That can't be right!" I said a little louder than I wanted to.

"I didn't get infected until well after this thing got out of control. I got bit by some-one else, I couldn't be part of the cause. Something is wrong with the equipment or the lab machines have been cross contaminated!" I said as I started to ramble, thinking of any reasonable slip-up that could've occurred.

Dr. Chavan sat there occasionally shaking his head ever so often in disagreement. I was beginning to get a little angry.

"Only a few people are working your samples and I've run them myself to verify." he said simply.

I started to speak again but he cut me off, which was a little out of his usual behavior.

"The lack of updated equipment may be an issue but the basic techniques never change. I don't have time to fully explain everything now but I need you to use your discretion and act like you know nothing for now. I promise you they still need you because you're still alive and talking. That has to count for something." he said quickly.

"Would you be willing to bet your own life on it?" I said as I smirked and suddenly coughed without warning. I was able to cover my mouth with my hand just in time but right after I noticed a few fine drops of blood in my palm as I pulled it away. Dr. Chavan saw my reaction and without hesitation he quickly took my hand by the wrist to see what it was. He looked into my already bloodied irises and shook his head, smirked in a playful manner and said, "You're just falling apart aren't you?"

It wasn't something I would've joked about.

The doctor was up in a second to hand me a box of *Kleenex* while I started to lecture him about infection control. He was close enough to where droplets could be an issue– at least from where I was trained it was a concern. He still had his disposable gloves on from earlier but shrugged off any real concern. He said that the virus itself and the infection statistics abroad made no suggestion about an airborne threat. Of course this brought me no comfort. Everything was trial and error these days with the exception that an error could cost someone and a lot of others their lives. I wasn't about to let up on the issue and set on to continue my point, if anything I would be the world's most conscientious dead-one. A swipe of the keycard on the outside sounded and the door opened quickly from Mia who whispered a quick and anxious, "They're coming!" before she closed the door just as quickly and was back on the outside of the room pretending to *not* inform us of their arrival.

The doctor looked at me in an anxious manner from where he was standing and before he could say anything more I pledged my secrecy. I remember my first night here when he said he would help me.

Aside from the warning, the sound of the door opening still managed to startle us both as Dr. Chavan now had my paper chart in his hands and was jotting a few things down when he hesitated. I remained seated on the couch with the tissues in hand as I looked to see who all was coming in. It was Dr. Strauss with my Uncle, another person from the lab– I presume from their lab coat, and Davenport along with another guy from security I recognized from before. The room seemed much smaller now with seven of us in it– not to mention Mia who peeked around the door while it was still open. We caught each other's eye and she gave me a supportive nod before she disappeared behind the shoulder of Davenport who eyed me with obvious suspicion and scrutiny. I was sure as the Head of Security he'd been briefed about the incident seconds after it happened. Any tiny bit of optimism and comfort I had remaining disappeared when my eyes met his. I was immediately more uncomfortable and automatically glanced down to his hands, expecting perhaps to see his firearm drawn already. To my surprise it wasn't, however the grey metallic, large caliber pistol was nearby in the holster attached to his belt.

I would've expected my Uncle to approach me first but it was Dr. Strauss who spoke to me. She looked concerned but seemed a bit refreshed and more youthful than before— maybe because her hair was now in a ponytail and she had on casual clothes; jeans and a Cornell University sweatshirt. She looked at least five years younger than my first estimation when I saw her and now appeared to be in her late-thirties. My uncle was still in similar attire as before; slacks, shirt and tie.

"Seanna, can you recall anything during the incident?" she said with a little alarm in her voice.

So that's what they were calling it now— 'the incident'. Interesting I thought.

"No, I don't remember anything. I was told I might've tried to attack the nurse, Mia which I wouldn't willfully do." I said as I ran my fingers through my hair. I felt embarrassed at this point and in a childlike manner, I let my hair fall and cover most of my face with the rest of it being covered by my hands— which seemed a little thinner. I was sure I would have to repeat everything I already told the others, along with the sincerest of apologies. The guard next to Davenport spoke out of nowhere, besides being rude it took me by surprise.

"I see we have the world's first polite and unintentional walker." he said in snide manner, just above a whisper to Davenport. He was at least four inches shorter and had to lean up into his ear to say it but nevertheless I heard it.

"Oh— go to hell, you have *no* idea what you're talking about!" I lashed out at him before several other voices jumped in. I heard my Uncle and Dr. Strauss trying to tell everyone to remain calm. I managed to shout out, "You just want to shoot at something!" before everyone quieted down again. Davenport told the guard to stand outside and gave him a gentle pat on the shoulder as he left. The guard was visibly upset but obeyed the request but left without another word. Dr. Chavan broke the tension by reporting off some of the saturation levels he told me about earlier. He saved me the trouble by recounting the incident the way it happened. He looked directly at me when he got to the part about my approaching Mia after she found me in the bathroom.

"I don't want to be restrained again." I said as soon as I felt the doctor was close enough to the end— the part where I was injected and soon after was dumbfounded about being on the floor with lots of protected hands, restraining me.

"Unfortunately, there may not be another option." Dr. Strauss said.

"Maybe we will increase the potency or give injections more frequently. They will do whatever they can, Seanna." Lloyd spoke up.

The mini-conference went on for about a minute more and they decided on more frequent injections until they could create something more potent. Until then, the schedule went from every four hours to every two with round the clock checks, every forty-five minutes and Mia along with every other nurse working with me had to have a second person with them when they came to check on me. Security would also be nearby. We all knew this would be a huge drain on resources but the only other option would be to join the other dead-ones in their section down in the lab.

No way.

I may almost be a dead-one but the person I am right now begged to differ. I felt the fatigue coming on and stood up only to make myself more comfortable on the couch. I laid my head down on one of the couch pillows which was more comfortable than it actually looked. Everyone else in the room stood back, a little startled themselves anxious to see what it was I was doing. Dr. Chavan double checked the time on his watch as they all confirmed the next several injection times.

"I'm think I'm gonna stay on the couch this time. That bed is bad luck." I said to the group.

"That's perfectly okay, you make yourself comfortable. None of us can fully comprehend what you are going through now." Lloyd replied.

Mia brought in bottled water with some fresh ginger ale already poured in a glass, bubbling. The sound was simple but soothing. The coolness of the water was soothing to my throat and hit my stomach like a rock but at this point it was more than a welcome event because I was doing something that the dead-ones didn't do. They had an appetite for live flesh. They were the cause of massive amounts of death even when they weren't gaining numbers. They weren't working together in a joint effort either—which was stunning. Each one worked for their own unending desires to attack and eat any and all who moved and they were happy to attack and eat the same person at once.

I wanted more of the cool water.

Chapter Ten

I couldn't have been more than five years old. It was the Fall season because most of the leaves were bright orange, yellow and red. I wasn't yet in my heaviest coat. I was in kindergarten when my mother suddenly showed up in class to excuse me from school early. She was carrying my brother who was just a toddler in her arms. He was fidgeting and trying to get down to be amongst the activities the other children in class were a part of. I was sitting with a few of my classmates at a round table and we were coloring trees using what we thought were supposed to be Fall colors only- that was what the teacher said to do. My mother was in a rush and I couldn't finish because I had a doctor's appointment that she told my teacher she was running late to make it to. Once we were outside my mother was talking to herself; or at least not to me or my brother as she buckled him into his car seat while I climbed into the backseat to sit on the other side. I heard her say, "This will be the last time –I promise," a few times under her breath before I asked her what she meant. She replied, "Nothing sweetheart, just make sure your seatbelt is buckled for me," before she reached over and checked it herself. During the car ride I rambled on about a cartoon character I saw on TV regularly, how they had magical powers and how no one could beat them. I remember asking her if anyone we knew had magical powers. The next thing I knew we arrived at a building I had been to before but was not the doctor's office at all. At the doctor's office you get a sticker or some crayons and a coloring book. These people were nice to me, though my mother never smiled while we were there. They'd let me measure myself- or at least try to. They asked me to sit still for as long as I could and how high I could count to. The next thing I remember I was back home and watching TV with the character that had superpowers again.

I slept through most of the afternoon on the couch, waking only to get another injection and to basically verify with the staff that I was still alive. Although the term 'sleeping like the dead' now had a whole new meaning, I was still more like the old fashioned meaning because I didn't move an inch during either nap. Mia was extremely brave- she wanted to be present for every dose and check-up while she was on duty. She came in with Louise who was still a bit shaken up from our last encounter. I couldn't blame her one bit. They both used extreme caution, saying my name gently to alert me, versus a traditional tap on the shoulder or leg. I bet being startled was not a catalyst to turning into a dead-one but it was smart to not jolt awake an infected person either.

Dr. Chavan returned eventually- I assume after he had some rest. By then, the daylight in the room was beginning to fade and more lights were being left on. He asked me about my appetite and I was completely honest with him. I was starving. It brought me to life to even discuss the topic.

"You know in Allentown- where I'm from, they have this excellent hoagie and pizza shop- Emma Lou's. Doc, I'm telling you- you want a good hoagie any way you like, they'd make it. They had the best pepperoni and sausage, like it was made by an Italian goddess or something. You could smell the bread dough and all the herbs from the parking lot," I explained with passionate detail and memory.

"If I could go back right now and order something it would be the Momma's Little Monster combo. That was the pepperoni and sausage hot hoagie with sautéed onions, peppers and a little lettuce. There'd be just enough of the thick sauce so it wouldn't leak out everywhere. I'd take it home for dinner if I had a late shift. They knew me as well as most of the other paramedics in the area . . . I hope they're doing okay and are safe somewhere," I said, coming back to the current reality.

The doctor listened to me and chuckled as I described to him this beautiful, edible work of art that was a part of my menu most weeks. He responded by telling me about his favorite restaurant that served traditional Indian cuisine as well as American food, saying they had the best curried tilapia and saffron chicken, as if it came from his mother's kitchen. A somber feeling overcame my ravenous hunger as I thought about his mother and all the other people I never knew and would never meet. Not because our paths would never cross on an ordinary day but now because there was an infection with a near one-hundred percent mortality rate that would prevent any sort of casual or friendly meetings, even by chance.

"Well there isn't any Emma Lou's on the menu but I bet we can do turkey and cheese." he said with a little optimism.

"If they don't have Saffron Chicken, then I'll take it." I said.

I meant it as he went on with the real reason why he was here. He seemed a bit anxious but I assumed it was for all of the obvious reasons. Our brief conversation about food had to show I was still very human because I saw on the television back at my place how the dead ones had no recollection or feelings- much less the desire to articulate anything beyond a mumble or groan. He looked into my eyes again with the pen light and took my temperature and pulse. Again, the vitals were both impossibilities to have and yet still be alive.

"Any better?" I asked him as soon as he could gather results.

"Not any worse. I'd say what we're doing now is effective." he replied. He moved quickly however, to make sure I wouldn't fall behind on my medication schedule. He told me this round would just be the anti-viral alone since the mixture with narcotic pain medication would probably start decreasing my appetite. I could tell I had lost a few pounds because the medium-sized threads I was in hung more loosely. It wasn't a diet I'd recommend by any means. As soon as Louise came in, he told her about the sandwich request and she picked up the phone. Louise already broke the rule about having two people in the room with me by leaving— though it was Dr. Chavan who sent her out of the room. Mia showed up and stood by his side. As he sat in the chair on the side of me I could see her giving him a caring massage on his shoulders. Louise was happy to go get the food— it was clear she didn't want to stay any longer than she had to.

The water on the coffee table was room temperature by now as the condensation left a ring around the bottom. I reached for the cup and let the soothing water fill my throat with gulps that made a louder than usual sound. They both waited in silent observation before he whispered quickly, "The deterioration has slowed considerably since this morning."

"That's awesome!" she replied.

"We could use some good news around here." he added.

"Speaking of news, do you think— . . . " she started to say before he cut her off with a sudden shake of his head. By then my cup was back on the table and they had my complete attention.

"What is it?" I said looking to both of them for a response.

"What news?" I said louder. I was beginning to get nervous, they just said I was doing better or at least that I had stop deteriorating which was better than not stopping so the news had to be about someone other than me.

"Oh come on, don't start this crap again, please— I can't take it!" I complained.

The doctor stared at the table in front of us and nodded his head. It was easy to see that it was a big decision for him to make, whether or not he should disclose this news to me. It had to be incredibly important because Mia was willing to spill the information, but only with his permission. I caught Mia's sly move, that the only way to get the ball rolling was to announce that they were hiding something in the first place. We were there in silence for only seconds longer when Dr. Chavan made his decision.

"Your condition has attracted a lot of attention around here at the facility. With the few hundred people residing here now, it was only a matter of time— I guess. The few people who've been working with your samples are all professional. I trust they would keep their promise to maintain your information in strict confidence." he said in a low tone.

"I know how it is, doctor, but what's the problem?" I asked him.

"The problem is ethical. For a potentially very valid reason your uncle believes you are the source of a vaccine that can be created. The problem is, two days after you arrived last week the trucks carrying all of the more sophisticated and valuable lab equipment on its way here went missing or was destroyed in all of the chaos right outside of Camden. He was counting on equipment because it would've been able to produce a vaccine right here at this facility," he said.

"My uncle was on the ball I guess– after all, this kind of stuff is right up his alley," I said.

"It's scary just how much. From his behaviors I'm guessing he is beginning to realize that keeping you here may not be the best idea. Even if we are able to maintain your current conditions or even cure you altogether, which would be a miracle– the resources here are limited. I think, and this is only from what I've suspected– that he is going to negotiate a deal to get you to another functioning lab facility," Dr. Chavan said. I could see the anticipation in his eyes for my reaction.

"Where would I go? The CDC? The World Health Organization headquarters? That sounds like a great idea to me," I questioned. If there was something I could do to help save lives, including my own while in the utmost secure location– I was all for it. I was ready to leave yesterday if that's the case.

The doctor shook his head again. "It's not either of those places."

"Why not?" I asked.

"You'll have to pardon my frankness but your uncle has become somewhat arrogant these last few years. I haven't known him for as long but his reputation precedes him in the science world. So much that he's made a few enemies in places most people would try to do the opposite. Especially at the CDC and FDA. Before now, he'd be lucky if they'd give him the time of day. Under the circumstances and the fact that he has you– I doubt he even has them on the phone list," Dr. Chavan pointed out so clearly.

I knew my uncle was something else. After my cousin Paige died he basically became his work. He knew of no other life outside of it. His own son, my cousin Nathan became bitter towards him because he felt like his father abandoned the family. At first we all thought it was grief that kept him away but there was this component of regret underneath that drove him into his work. I hadn't seen him in years, since my cousin Paige's funeral. Before that tragic time, it was once or twice a year at the most we would see him at family functions. Most years it was not at all.

For the first time, someone outside of the family was verifying this. At first, I wanted to defend my uncle because he was my family and I remember the grief we all endured because of Paige's sudden, tragic death. It may have been a rumor but I heard that my uncle was supposed to pick her up from the library that fateful evening but a miscommunication inevitably put her on the sidewalk right as a car veered off of the road. There was no bad weather, no one to blame but a careless driver who was perhaps texting or drunk. To make things worse, no one stepped forward and no one nearby the accident scene could give an accurate description of the vehicle. There was only blue paint and common tire tracks from what was most likely a larger model sedan.

"Did he burn his bridges so bad that they wouldn't work with him now, even in a crisis?" I said.

"Maybe, maybe not. Either way he's made it clear to us he's not willing to discuss anything going on here, even when it's his ethical duty to do so- even with the survival of humanity at stake,"

So my uncle had gone a little rogue in the last few years. It was definitely not like him to break the rules but then again if he was doing something that bad, why didn't his superiors discipline him? I thought about some of the possible reasons why he'd managed to avoid serious consequences and corruption came to mind but I had a much smaller pond I wanted to fish from. Since we were all being so honest right now I figured I would push things a little further.

"Why won't he allow me to see my parents or my boyfriend?" I asked. I looked at Mia hoping she'd get that I wouldn't tell her part in the unsuccessful search of my mother and father, nor would I disclose the favor she granted me of bringing Graham to my room days ago. Not seeing either of them in so long was beginning to give me more fear and anxiety.

"I've not actually seen your parents here so I don't understand why he's telling you that. Maybe it's purely for your cooperation. Maybe Dr. Burges feels he will actually find them for you, still." he said.

"I guess there's a point to you telling me all of this- so why?" I said, as I noticed I was becoming fatigued now.

"You're right, there is. I- we think the right thing to do is for you to go to one of the government run agencies, or a research hospital- one that is still functioning. We have done right by you so far in treating your injuries and attempting to stabilize the progression of the virus to our own amazement. It's time to pass on what we know to a facility that's more equipped and will do the best they can ethically and honestly. We're trying to discreetly get in touch with several facilities we think are still capable but communication is difficult at times, you know that." The doctor said, glancing up at Mia occasionally to her obvious approval. I could figure out on my own that even with the lines of communication working, if it was true what Dr. Chavan just said about my uncle basically being blackballed from the science world, it would be difficult to get in touch with the right people- even on a day sans the current catastrophe. At the same time, it would be even more difficult for those people to get in touch with the right peo- ple here. The wrong person could find out and they'd be up in security's office in a matter of minutes.

"Okay, I get it. I'm on board. I know I don't want to be sold off to the highest bidder in the underground world of science and I don't like the lies being told to me either. You know I want to be kept informed. I've said that from the moment I woke up here." I told them both.

"Indeed, you have Seanna ..." he started to say but was cut off as the door opened and Louise cautiously walked in with a covered plate. It seemed she didn't know what to expect, perhaps she thought I'd be on the other side again by now. We all looked at her as she paused to get a look around and then quickly walked past Mia and the doctor to sit the plate down on the coffee table in front of me. She mentioned the sandwich was hot and that there were some graham crackers on the side along with apple slices. I sincerely thanked her and she welcomed me as best as she could but clearly she was plain scared still, I could tell. Once she left the room Dr. Chavan quickly got back to our discussion.

"I suspect you are on the same page with us but I need you to know also that things could possibly go in a different direction than any of us might anticipate. Would you be willing to take the chance at all?" he said in a more serious tone.

"I would, of course." I replied. I couldn't imagine a scenario any more scarier than what I've already been through. I've already concluded that this thing- whatever it is- is more than about me alone. I happen to be an outlier that can still make a difference in the equation.

"Okay. As long as this medication regiment is working we'll try to make as much of it as possible, discreetly of course. We'll keep you in the loop- as you say. Try and eat so you can begin to regain your strength. Mia and I will return in a little while to give you something for your pain," Dr. Chavan said as he got up and they both left.

I could tell that they both were pleased to find out I was in agreement with their plans. I don't know what my uncle was planning to do with me especially if he couldn't cure me. I always felt that it would be only a matter of time before Davenport raised his weapon at me and pulled the trigger with fatal results. If it weren't him it could easily be one of the even less forgiving guards like the one who was up in my room earlier. These guys no longer saw me as a human being- I knew this for sure. Maybe they'd even told Graham I had already died- which wouldn't surprise me one bit either since it was clear that my parents were not here which was the exact opposite of what my uncle told me, a couple times. Why would he repeatedly lie to me like that? I knew he was the only one who could answer that question.

CHAPTER ELEVEN

I didn't know what to expect whenever I woke up. All I knew was that I'd be groggy and that my body felt a little more than stiff for good reason. The last two days were routine since Dr. Chavan and Mia disclosed my uncle's questionable intentions for me and his thoughts on working up a vaccine for this monster of a virus I was told by now killed millions in the U.S alone. I'd managed to not fully become one of the dead ones due to a very diligent medication schedule and more needle sticks than any one person would receive in a lifetime. Though Dr. Chavan failed to mention any more of what we discussed that afternoon two days ago, Mia was more forthcoming during her visits and would drop little suggestive statements like, "Everything seems to be lining up perfectly," and "Things are certainly looking better," as she would come in and out of my room.

My appearance seemed to improve ever so slightly. I don't know if it was my new and improved diet of sandwiches and vegetables or the medicine or both. I went from looking almost exactly like the undead with the grayish pale skin, grey-hue lips and sunken eyes to a more lively shade that made it seem as if I only needed some sun. Since I was able to keep down food I stopped losing weight and instead I managed to feel like I had some strength. The wounds I had on my shoulder and forearm were well into healing. They started to itch– which was a sign of repair, which was a sign of life. It seemed as if the pendulum was starting to swing back in the other direction. I failed to see hide nor hair of my uncle which was probably a good thing because the last few days brought the opportunity for me to reflect and become angry at all of the questions I had and the conclusions I had come to regarding my parents and his plans for me. It would be pretty hard for me to fake not knowing what I'd been told and the lies my uncle tried to placate me with. After all, I was the one who originally wanted out of this place and for lack of better effort, I was still here. If I had to do it again, I would perhaps include scaling the wall or armed grand theft auto as a part of the plan.

For now, I would wait for Dr. Chavan and Mia and let them make as much of the medication as possible until I could get to a real research facility— one that hasn't managed to be cast-off by the FDA or the CDC and all the other alphabets of importance, for starters.

The next time the door opened and Mia came in with Louise, I was in the bathroom again and although during the last few days poor Louise began to trust that I was not going to kill her, I may have just set them both back on edge. The water was running when they stepped in and I was washing my face and attempting to comb my freshly shampooed hair. I was fiddling around with the toothbrush cover and dropped the toothpaste which made enough noise and was unrecognizable. I didn't hear either of them come into the room, nor did I see them until I'd come out of the bathroom toothbrush- in- mouth and scared the crap out of both of them. They scared the crap out of me as well because by then Mia had already grabbed a metal vase that came from off of one of the shelves on the TV stand. Poor Louise was already by the door ready to take off and yell for help. My simple walk out of the bathroom almost set off a sequence of bad events.

"Holy hell you scared us Seanna! You didn't hear me calling you?" Mia said as she lowered the vase and gave me a big, spontaneous hug. I kind of froze as she accidently bumped me in the back with the object that could've easily been planted in my skull by now.

"No, I couldn't hear you— I was washing my face and brushing my teeth. The water feels so good," I said, mouth full of paste, eventually patting her back in return.

"I have some good news for you Seanna— they're almost ready, it'll only be another day or two. They wanted me to let you know. Looks like you'll be going to Princeton!" Mia said excitedly.

I gave Louise a nervous glance before I said anything more. Mia was anxiously awaiting my reaction before she figured out why I was so hesitant.

"It's okay, she's knows— she's okay with it and wants to help, right Louise?" Mia said quickly in an attempt to minimize doubt.

My mouth still filled with toothpaste and all almost hit the floor after hearing the news. I couldn't believe it with Louise being so timid and apprehensive toward me. Maybe Louise had a bigger heart than I could tell. Louise responded with a half crooked smile and nodded her head slightly. I said nothing as I went back into the bathroom before I lost all of the now extra sudsy toothpaste.

"We've made contact with several researchers at the University's laboratory. They're pretty eager to get a look at you for themselves, personally. We're going to transfer all that we have about this virus along with your info in a secure file to them while the internet is still partially functioning. We've got enough medicine and anti-viral to last you at least a week right now, that way they can replicate it and modify it on their own as well. I got a good feeling about this! They can even begin to test it on any infected people before they succumb to it," Mia rattled on with so much optimism.

"That sounds really great! When do we leave?" I said, now that my mouth was rinsed.

"That's our biggest obstacle— the how and when part. It'll probably be at night of course— possibly tomorrow night. Getting you out of the room and down to a car will be a challenge, even at night with all of the lighting and staff on guard. When anything comes or goes it's a big deal, here," Mia said.

"You've got to figure out a way to get Graham with us too," I said.

Mia looked a little helpless and said nothing. I could tell she was thinking.

"Hey, there's no way I'm getting separated from him. You can't possibly ask me to leave here without him, no way!" I said, shaking my head in protest. I was already separated from him. I thought about our brief time in his basement when he said he'd be with me until the end. There was not a snowball's chance I'd leave him here and go to any other location. Besides, I know my uncle would be infuriated by my abrupt and secretive departure. How could I leave my boyfriend here to deal with the backlash? They'd assume he was in on everything. Graham was smart and could hold his own but he'd be way outnumbered here.

"We are still working out the details my darlin' so just sit tight okay?" Mia said, giving me a hardy pat on the shoulder. Just then I remembered an old Robert Burns quote I heard Mrs. Schuler, one of my English teachers in high school repeat, "The best laid plans of mice and men often go astray." Thinking about the whole poem now, compared to mice, even men are shaken.

"Okay, but I'm not going anywhere without him. That's the deal breaker." I warned.

After they took care of their usual business of checking my vitals and injections, Mia and Louise left again but returned quickly as they surprised me with something extra special. It was now closing in on dinnertime. Apparently they heard of my appetite for Italian and had lasagna prepared which wasn't half bad. It was filled with Italian sausage, little bits of onion and the ricotta cheese was perfectly seasoned and blended with parmesan. It came with a simple tomato and cucumber salad and breadstick which was a feast altogether as far as I was concerned. I was grateful for their thoughtfulness— it almost brought me to tears and it seemed they were both happy to see me smile. After they assured me there was plenty left for everyone else in the building, they left to enjoy the food for themselves; Mia gave me another quick hug and told me she'd see me tomorrow and that Louise would return later with someone else.

I noticed I was always left alone to eat which I was not entirely used to. Graham and I always ate dinner together at least four or five nights a week unless I picked up an extra shift like in the days before all hell broke loose when I was on the tail end of an eight day stretch. Lately we'd always spend equal amounts of time between both of our places, especially whenever Darin or Chad was entertaining the ladies at their house. Graham was acting less and less like a bachelor which was a great sign for our relationship. Sometimes he'd come to my place for a couple days whenever he had a presentation or something important to work on. Now, I missed his regular conversation, I missed his touch and running my hands through his beautiful golden brown hair and looking into his brownish green eyes. I was having a moment, I knew it and within a few seconds food wasn't the only thing I wanted to enjoy but both appetites grew colder thinking about the path that lay ahead for both of us. Wherever I was going so was he, I would make it happen.

On an oddly pleasant note, it was nice to know that I was still able to feel some of the more human emotions. Heaven only knows I wanted to be with Graham right now and forever afterward. I stood up from the couch, leaving the majority of the food on the plate and walked over to the window. Slight pains erupted in me all over as I looked out into the sunlight restricted view of thick forest and wild vegetation that was at least as far as the window view. The sun had only minutes left in the day and there wasn't much to see past all of the trees and the incoming darkness. I could only hope the dead ones wouldn't be out wandering this far into nothingness. I didn't know how far away from the city this place was but it seemed it would take days for anyone to get here on foot. Who knows, according to the word I received, maybe tomorrow I'd get a chance to see just how far, for myself.

The pain medication couldn't have come any sooner as my comfort quickly decreased and I spent my last few minutes awake chatting with Louise about the facility's location. She was now with me alone after one of the armed guards opened the door first, of course.

"Princeton U is in Princeton, New Jersey." Louise chuckled a little.

"No, that's not what I meant. Where are we now?" I said lazily.

"Oh, ha! As you young folks say 'my bad', I'm sorry. We're just outside of Medford Lakes . . . New Jersey." Louise said with a smile.

I figured as much. I knew we weren't far from my uncle's home and judging from the apparent peace and quiet of the environment, we were well off the beaten path-otherwise like the dead ones, there would be mobs of people trying to get in, overwhelming any safe location like I saw on TV and heard about. I was sure the armed men here could handle wanderers from both the alive and dead variety because they had the both the manpower and fire power. It would have been a bloodbath by now if we were within the city limits of Camden or Philadelphia across the way.

"Does this mean you're not afraid of me anymore?" I asked Louise.

"It's not you by any means . . . I'm sure just like me, you've seen the infection get a hold and take down people you love." She replied. Quickly, it was beginning to take some effort for her to restrain her emotion.

"You're right." I said.

"There's no comparing anymore because the lists are too long for the dead and missing. There's nothing but devastation- on a human level. It's not like a natural disaster where the biggest mess is damage to property where fatalities are isolated and the path of destruction is obvious. They can't just dispatch help to the scene, fix it up and pray it never happens again." Louise said.

"I know, believe me I'm worried about more than just myself," I told her with the deepest sincerity.

"You can't believe how it feels to have this vicious virus lingering in my veins. To be infected and alive from it is almost worse than actually dying. I feel suspended, you know— stuck between life and death and in the meantime everyone who knows is afraid of me. They don't mean to show it but whenever they walk in here I'm sure they're afraid of what they may find." I gave her the absolute truth.

"I'm sorry— I know it must be hard. You're managing the best way you can." Louise patted me on the shoulder like Mia did earlier.

Aided by the effects of the drugs, I relaxed completely into the mattress of the bed. I wanted instead to be concerned about the impending travel plans as there should be concern for the safe travels of moving to any location. The apparent collapse of every system we generally took for granted a short time ago was good enough reason for extreme caution. A quick glance on the wall confirmed eight o'clock.

Before I knew it, I was waking up to be poked again. Ten-thirty.

And again, two and a half hours later.

It was indeed like clockwork. I figured Louise was long gone as perhaps a minute or two went by when I felt someone was watching me. I must've been out like light because I didn't feel the bed move against the weight. Once I opened my eyes, it took only a split second to distinguish the figure sitting by my knees on the side of the bed. It was nothing but silence as I sat up quickly and Graham gently gave me a hug and commented on how much healthier I looked. "Be careful," I warned him, jumping straight into what concerned me the most. We embraced for a few seconds longer.

"We're going to be okay." Graham's soothing voice vibrated against my ear. I pulled back from him which I could tell made him wonder.

I was afraid I would accidently give him the virus, along with anyone else I got too close. I figured it wouldn't take a substantial bite with broken skin and tissue like I experienced. I was told it wasn't airborne but I wasn't about to take any chances. I looked past Graham to see who was here with him and was surprised to find he was here alone.

"I told them I would be your nurse from now on." Graham joked before he told me that out of nowhere Louise called his room and offered to try and sneak him here. He then told me that Louise overheard security saying that there were a few glitches in the cameras for the inside and how they were trying to get it fixed but it was unlikely they'd be up again soon because instructions were to conserve power with the generators.

"How are you?" I asked. I wasn't ready to tell him that I had literally died and been resuscitated, nor that I had begun to turn into a dead one but was stopped by my NGT's miracle recipe that worked only for me. Right now, I only cared about him and how he'd been the last few days. A few things were clear after our quick catch-up; they kept him busy and away from me purposefully and there was still no sign of either of my parents here. I was also shocked and curious when Graham said that one of the guys from security, whom I was sure was Davenport by description, seemed to take an interest in him, myself and our relationship.

"I don't know what's going on with him but he was definitely probing for something." Graham specifically said.

I would have to ponder more about Davenport's motives later but in the meanwhile I had to tell Graham the more important news. "We're leaving this place, hopefully tomorrow for the Princeton University Laboratory," I said bluntly. I was about to explode waiting the second or two it took to for him to respond. I never really saw him get amped up about anything except Division I basketball where he, Chad and Darin were pretty much super fans. I remember spending many hours with them in front of the fifty-one inch plasma screen that they all chipped in to buy. I searched his face, particularly his eyes as he looked down at the floor, thinking.

"I figured they wouldn't be able to do as much here." he said undoubtedly.

"I'm surprised– it seemed like they had everything." I replied.

"To you and anyone else unfamiliar with scientific technology– I believe them when they said the better equipment didn't make it. Either way, you go– I go." Graham said. His confidence put me at ease. I needed it too. He rested his hand on my knee and smiled. He and I both knew how lucky we were to have made it this far.

Graham told me that in the past few days he'd help them set up greenhouses on the roof and how they would be okay without him because there were at least five other people with him at all times helping out. According to him, it was nothing but lumber, nails, plastic sheeting and within three days they had two separate gardens on one roof and one on another building. The dirt and seeds were in all the same day. May was the perfect time as the danger of frost was pretty much minimal by this time. He said he was confident the full sun would bring them edible crops quickly. I looked into his eyes as he talked and occasionally his lips as they moved. Every movement he made caused me to smile and feel even warmer inside my heart. I believed at this point he was made for these kinds of moments when survival was questionable. He was not naturally rugged looking like he'd spent most of his time outdoors but his knowledge of agriculture and science combined, oddly seemed more than enough to get everyone through this atrocity. For now, it would be enough to get us through.

I told Graham there was no set time of departure yet, but to be ready at a moment's notice. I told him that Mia or Louise would give him any updates and that Dr. Chavan was going to make sure that I had enough antiviral with me to make it there and then some. How we got to the university was going to be another issue that needed to be worked out. The door opened just then, startling us both– Graham tensing up for perhaps whatever but it was just Louise who said a quick, "It's time to wrap this up, we gotta get you back to the other area."

It was me this time who reached out for him. I hugged him, this time squeezing as hard as I could. Just like any other time his hands felt great on my back. I took in deep breaths to help control my emotions– becoming sadder than ever at his necessary departure. I went through hell after the last time he left. He promised it would be much sooner the next time he'd see me and that I was all he would think about until then. He gave me another quick kiss, told me to be strong and went away with Louise who was in a hurry to get him back to his building.

I was no longer tired after that injection. I leaned on my good shoulder and spent at least an hour worrying about all the possible things that could go wrong– which were plenty. What if Princeton didn't live up to their claims they could help? What if they just wanted me so they could see for themselves how long I would live? My uncle was quite possibly all I had left for family which took my thoughts down a different path and I was soon angered again by the apparent lies he told about my parents being here. I'd rather spend the time left in my life looking for them and my brother for the sake of finding out if they were okay. My mind switched back to the equally challenging task of getting out of here to begin with. I'd try to convince them all to come. We could have a van full of people. Mia, Dr. Chavan, Louise, Ruben, along with Graham and I– all had tickets to get out of here, paid in full as far as I was concerned. I knew in my heart however, that the more people involved, the riskier it would be for everyone to get away safely and that was just getting out of the gates. Beyond that we would probably be in even more trouble.

Chapter Twelve

he morning started early. It was barely sunrise and six-thirty when things got moving. After my mind and body decided they had about all of the rest they required under the excitement of the forthcoming events, I rolled out of bed to ready myself. I washed my face and did all of the usual grooming- put my hair in a bun and brushed my teeth. I did this all very slowly, though the will was there to get it done quickly. From the window I saw the clouds pressed heavily together creating an oppressive and dense atmosphere that was full with moisture, ready to fall- I could feel the humidity radiate through the walls. Dr. Chavan and Mia were preceded by a guard again before they came into the room. Mia toted a small Rubbermaid cart that had the usual supplies they needed however as soon as they both were inside and the door was closed, she pulled out a small black bag that reminded me of a carry-on bag for a plane ride.

"We need to hide this in here until it's time to go. You absolutely cannot leave here without it." Mia instructed. The doctor was obviously distracted by something because he remained quiet. He stood by the cart, this time grabbing the tourniquet supplies and tubes for the usual blood draw.

"What's in there?" I asked Mia.

"A week's worth of anti-viral, close to eighty doses including a few for the university to use for replication. All are premeasured in syringes with needles. There are various pain medications in pill and syringe form: Percocet, Dilaudid and a broad spectrum antibiotic all labeled separately along with first aid supplies. We were debating about putting in another port for you to make it easier but you're a medic anyways, you know what to do."

"Yeah, you might want to consider the port... Wouldn't want to catch a deadly infection," I said sarcastically.

The doctor came over and put his stethoscope to my chest which immediately cued our silence. Understandably, it took him longer to get a steady, countable heart beat. He then used his pen light and flashed it quickly into my eyes.

"The hemorrhaging around your irises has improved somewhat since the last time

I checked- this is good," he commented.

I was told this was all a part of a quick physical examination to make sure I was 'fit for travel'- which under the circumstances, I found to be incredibly funny. We all shared a little laugh after I told him I found this to be amusing. I doubt any of us wanted me to stay here any longer regardless but he said if I weren't up to it, he'd postpone everything. It was obvious while he was testing me that some things were worse than any normal physical I had. It could've been due to my being bedridden for the last week or the effects of the virus and meds but I was noticeably weaker, off balance and more easily exhausted. I hoped during my departure I didn't have to run any long distance because it might certainly change the outcome.

"Of course I'd love to see you healthier when the time comes for your departure- but that's a redundant statement under the circumstances. I'm one hundred percent positive you will have a better chance there. Unless things change, I give you the okay." The doctor wrote down a few things on my paper chart.

"I think so too," Mia added.

They didn't have to tell me- they had me at '*better equipment*'.

"You guys are coming too, right? You two should be there with me. We can all go together." I begged.

"As much as I'd like to, I feel a responsibility to my colleagues here. I can't aban-don them." Dr. Chavan answered, crushing my hopes for a group exodus.

I already knew Mia wouldn't separate from him. If the situation were switched, I wouldn't leave Graham either. I looked away not out of sadness, because I completely understood where they were coming from. I looked away to think about how Graham and I would make it out of here, alone.

"So what's the plan? One of you pull the fire alarm while I duck out of the back door?" I said, wishing it would be that easy. I knew nothing about the layout of the property and I doubt there would be a car waiting for us with the keys inside. This was going to take work- calculations, knowledge of NGT's operations and a lot of luck in our favor to get out of here. Making it all the way to Princeton would be a miracle.

Dr. Chavan paid attention to Mia who started in on the instructions. She unfolded sheet of paper and began to draw with her pen, blocks that were representations of buildings. I could easily remember seeing the same thing from when I was transported to this building. Luckily, there was a back door to this place which was locked electron-ically and the easiest way to get through she figured, was to actually get a hold of someone's card key. She figured in the aftermath and questioning that would follow after my 'successful departure' it would be a good idea to have someone's else card other than hers or the doctor's.

"We'll do our best to keep the peace here afterward so they don't find out where you've gone, we'll keep quiet about all of that." Mia said confidently.

"Make sense to me. So you'll sneak Graham over here to me again?" I said, asking her nervously.

"That's the plan- after dark. When he shows up that's the cue things are in motion," she replied.

She continued to draw a few other smaller boxes on the piece of paper. She drew a large 'X' over the building signifying the one we were in. So far there were three large boxes and two smaller boxes. Mia told me that this was definitely not to scale but the two smaller buildings were on the opposite side of where we were. The diagram of the boxes looked like a square with our building being the southernmost building. The two smaller buildings, one of which was unfinished and used for storage was nearby would be easier to go there versus the other building directly across from it. The main building was Northernmost, which I was in before and security's main office was there. The second smallest building— the garage, was located farther north on the map, from the storage building and northwest from the main building. The trickiest part would be getting past the main building and beyond the guarded, wrought-iron perimeter gates.

Instead of remaining focused on the difficult part of getting out, Mia continued on, giving directions to Princeton.

"Assuming the interstate is not the best route we think it'll be better following these directions. It's only forty miles from here on a normal day but a couple extra miles to stay out of harm's way seems reasonable to me," she said.

She whipped out another piece of paper with written instructions from here to the campus science facilities— which were easy to read and understandable. From my line of work I was used to following directions especially my first year on the job. Since the ambulances have yet to be fitted with GPS that allows them to get from one location to another versus just for locating purposes I became an expert at following mapped instructions.

"This seems cool, I should be able to get to the garage— no problem." I said, after a moment of skimming through the neat handwriting.

She explained to me for simplicity, the keys to all of the vehicles, both those belonging to personnel and NGT, hung on hooks which corresponded to the numbered spots the vehicles were parked in. Around ten-thirty the security personnel changes shift for the night. There are more guards at night but the priority lies in protecting the perimeter than the goings on within the buildings. It would be after we were leaving the garage that Louise will announce my 'missing' status— to decrease the chance that they would shoot to kill, thinking we were complete strangers. It was now when Mia informed me that Davenport was reprimanded by my uncle for the possibility of using deadly force in the hallway back at the main building days ago. It was Dr. Strauss who gave him the tranquilizer gun under my uncle's strict instructions to keep me alive.

Mia put a lot of effort into giving me all the necessary details. For that, I would give this the best shot I could attempt. Come nightfall, I would be ready. I'd follow the instructions exactly and within forty miles or so, I would again be in a safe place. I told Mia I intended on seeing her and the doctor again. It was hard to fathom these being the last few times I would see them both. I owed it humanity to try and bring us back from the brink of extinction— it freaked me out to again acknowledge our dire state.

The rest of the morning went by in a routine manner. I told Mia that I didn't want anything to minimize the pain because I wanted to be alert. Instead of spending the day intermittently sleeping, I spent a lot of time looking out of the window, rehearsing different scenarios in my mind and trying to resolve them before they became realistic. Mia arrived in her usual timing and added a few extra items to the bag- including the painkillers I would've normally taken. She also dropped in a stethoscope, a digital timer watch, and a few alcohol pads that she forgot to include earlier. I understood the need to keep track of these in case it took longer than a few hours to get there. Though it would probably take more than an hour, there was no harm in being prepared for delay.

When lunchtime arrived, I received a half of a plate of carrots and celery with salad dressing and ginger ale. I tried to eat as much of it as possible thinking that it would maybe even help my complexion to gain a little more healthy color as well as for energy later on. Dr. Chavan as well as Dr. Strauss came up to the room soon after. I knew right away when they walked in that the game was still on because of the obvious nontruths that were being reported.

"She's been tolerating her current levels of anti-viral and pain medication well today," he said, even though I'd already gone two times without pain medication.

Dr. Strauss looked me over, seemingly satisfied with my improvements. I managed to sit on the couch and pretend to be exhausted when instead internally I was revving up for the evening. My pain was slowly starting to return but I wasn't about to let it spoil the occasion. It felt like my muscles were becoming extremely sore but it was more subtle this time. I purposefully chose not to say anything because for starters, I was a terrible liar. The first time she asked me something that I was sure I'd have to cover- my eyes would probably give it away. The two chatted about my uncle and how they were discovering other previously unknown centers that were on this newly setup survivor's database that was partially electronic and partially on sign posts and setup throughout the area. This was exciting to hear and gave me a great deal of hope inside. Though I tried not to perk up at the positive development, my full attention was clinging to every bit of information.

By nightfall, I was nearly boiling over in anticipation and pacing the floor of the medium sized room. Mia told me the plan was to leave at nightfall- though she failed to mention exactly when. When I wasn't pacing, I spent a lot of time at the narrow window looking out of it, searching. It was as if that window's view to the outside had all the answers to my questions. Graham's arrival to my room would signal everything's 'a-go' I was told, so by the third time the door opened for various other reasons I was about ready to have a heart attack.

Another familiar and friendly face showed up to this room. I was already acquainted with Ruben, the janitor from the main building. He pulled his cart into my room, humming some slow but familiar tune in the process. We greeted each other with warm smiles, though he waited until the door was fully closed before he spoke.

"How are you sweetheart? Don't mind them- they are bored and nosey as hell." he said of the armed personnel that preceded him into the room.

"I'm doing better now, Ruben– thanks," I said.

"I heard you had it rough for a while but you're tough, everyone can see that– you're still here." he said in an assuring tone.

I wish I felt as confident as he sounded.

"I've seen better days but you're right, I'm still here," I agreed.

"Well, for now you are," he responded with a sly look in his eyes.

This struck me as an odd reaction from him until he reached under the shelves of his cart, pulled out a medium plastic bag and handed it to me.

"I had to do something for you– it's nothing special. I understand you're leaving tonight," he mumbled in a low tone.

My mouth dropped in surprise as I took the bag, opened it and looked at its contents. Inside there was a pair of jeans, a blue, t-shirt and a matching hooded zip-up sweatshirt.

"Thank you *so* much for this! They're the right size and everything– wow! So you know, too?" I said with a mix of excitement and concern. I didn't pause as I put the shirt and pants up to my body and legs, satisfied that it was a perfect match to my size.

"I told you– you remind me of my niece. Unfortunately I haven't heard from her to find out if she's okay. They were supposed to be a gift for her birthday last week but we all have much bigger problems now." he said with sadness and regret in his voice.

I immediately insisted that he take them back because even under the grave circumstances, I hoped he would find his niece and give these items to her like he originally intended. Through some miracle I hoped we all would recover from this event and find everyone we loved, alive and well. After a few seconds of further debate and his absolute stance, I kept the clothes and thanked him heartily. I gave him a hug– in which he did not recoil from. Come to think of it, his mannerisms reminded me of my mother's cousin, Larry. He was also similar in stature and personality– the way they made you feel like you'd known them for years after only a few conversations. Ruben smiled at me but I could see the concern in his eyes as well. Concern was something that we all had because everything that came our way was new at this point. Ruben looked in my eyes and after the few seconds it took for me to figure he was probably able to see the broken blood vessels, I turned away. It scared me to have someone else afraid of what I had no control over.

"I know you're good Seanna. You wouldn't hurt anyone on purpose– it's okay sweetheart. That's part of the reason why I'm going to help you get out of here." he said.

I didn't want him– or anyone for that matter, to risk their own safety as he'd done more than enough for me already just from being a kind person. I shook my head and was about to remind him of all the perfectly good reasons why he shouldn't be a part of my departure efforts. For starters, if you weren't infected and part of your uncle's seemingly seedy ulterior motives– this was a safe place. There was food, shelter and protection that no doubt only a few in the population outside of law enforcement and military had access to. I wasn't even remotely aware of any places like this before coming here and chances are, I would've been a dead one by now anyway— or a pile of human remains, either way. When they found me I was already in the middle of a fight to the death with a dead one in Graham's living room that left me with gaping bite wound on my forearm. Because of the circumstances, it continues to be truly in one's own best interest to be concerned with their own safety and if not, only those closest to you. From what I've heard, other people weren't taking half the chance outside of this place. Here was Ruben— this kind hearted man was throwing his self-right in the middle of harm's way by helping to get me out of here.

"I know it doesn't look like it, but I've been preparing myself for what's outside of here. I don't want it on my conscience to have you hurt or worse because of things that have nothing to do with you. Ruben, I'm sorry— I can't have that." I apologized.

He looked at me with no reaction in his face and simply replied, "It's my choice, believe me."

The door opened almost without either of us noticing. The conversation was so intense for me; I felt I had to convince this kind man that I didn't want him in harm's way. Mia should've been done with her shift for the night but she walked in and Graham was right behind her. We all exchanged glances and smiled but when I saw Graham we both ran up and hugged each other again. Seeing him again never got old with me. He held me for a longer than usual time. I said nothing and only nodded my head as he whispered in my ear, asking if I was okay and if I was ready.

At this point I was ready as I'd ever be.

I wanted to pay more attention to what Mia and Ruben were discussing. The two took the brief opportunity and stood off to the side whispering to each other while Graham inquired about the bag of medications and supplies that even he was warned we must never part with. I brought it to him and he quickly inspected the inside, nodded— seemingly satisfied with the contents. I noticed his fresh change of clothes and his now slightly darker, sun-kissed skin. He reached in his pocket and threw a couple of items into the bag. He smiled when I commented about his newly acquired tan. It was an ongoing joke between us. I'd always say we looked more like siblings than a couple when he spent a lot of time outside in the sun. Right now I realized that the joke wasn't as funny this time because now it was me who still looked pale, more than he was— for a very different reason.

"I'm gonna go get ready," I said as I took the bag Ruben gave me and headed into the bathroom. The shoes I had were sufficient but when I returned there was another slightly used pair of *New Balance* running shoes on the bed. I asked no questions and quickly put them on as Mia now talked with Graham. I hurried to hear what she was saying. By now Ruben had already left the room.

"Okay, you should have everything you need, in that bag. Remember, everywhere you go, this goes with you— even though I suppose it's equally important that you make it to the university in one piece," Mia said as she held up the bag.

Graham put his arm behind my back. I could feel his hand settle at my waist.

Knowing him, it was his nonverbal way of assuring me we were going to make it to our destination. Mia went over the instructions one last time about the medication schedule and the timer. She had another dose ready to give me right now and I took off the hoodie and exposed my upper arm for the shot. Graham immediately walked over to the bag, retrieved the timer and set the alarm to go off in three and a half hours. Mia said the Princeton lab was expecting us to arrive sometime tonight though she didn't provide them an exact time. Once we were on our way she'd try and let them know but she couldn't promise anything because of her obvious expected involvement in the search efforts here. It made perfect sense because she would be one of the last people to see me before her shift change, so of course my uncle and whoever else would want to talk to her.

While she was sharing this information I realized the juxtaposition she was now in because of her involvement with Dr. Chavan. He would have to question her and possibly put on quite a show to pretend to be unaware of the situation. Again, here was another individual who would have to take a great risk to see that I make it out of NGT. Mia handed me a keycard that belonged to another employee here. She also handed one to Graham that had the name of a different employee. She told us to use them both intermittently once we left here- so it would be harder to track either of them should things progress more quickly than expected.

Lastly, Mia gave us both a quick hug because the next time she saw us- if ever again, things would be hurried. She wished us the best of luck and I tried not to be sad about leaving her. I thanked her again and again for everything she did. Graham thanked her in return for everything and promised some sort of reciprocation when the opportunity availed itself. She gave us a playful wink and smiled but changed her tone immediately as she opened the door and hurried out of sight to get away from the area and back to wherever she'd normally be at this time of night. Mia disappeared around the corner behind the closing door. We were now alone as Graham carefully took my hand and guided me back to the couch.

For a few seconds there was silence as we sat together and my pale little fingers carefully caressed his back.

"Are you okay? I don't know about you but I'm nervous as hell right now." I said, exhaling with a little nervous chuckle.

"I know we've all had better days. We're gonna get there Seanna." he said.

"Graham, neither of us has been out there since we came here. How many days ago was that? What if things are really out of hand now? What if we break down somewhere and get trapped? What if we get separated? What if something happens that causes me to miss the injection on time- I don't want flip out again." I rambled on to him.

"We can't worry about what we have no control over. I know it's gonna be bad out there. We'll do what we need to- one thing at a time, we'll deal with it." he said.

"I haven't had any pain medication at all today. I want a clear head for whatever we encounter out there. Weird thing is, I think my adrenaline and nerves are keeping it at bay." I told him, knowing he was about to make a fuss over it. He started to object when I carefully grabbed his hand and put it up to my heart. It worked because he paused in silence to feel my heartbeat.

"See, this is still working. It's slow I know, and truthfully it hurts a lot– but I'm gonna make sure we both get there safely." I spoke to him. My heartbeat was still present, weak as it was– it still existed. I had chills and my extremities were impossibly cold since I came here. Painful as it was, I could handle all of those symptoms– it was becoming a dead one that I couldn't handle.

"I don't like the idea of you being in so much pain during all of this, but I understand." he said it in a way that I could tell he was assuring himself at the same time.

He wasn't far from the truth either. I was starting to hurt like a son of a bitch. I was just barely beginning to have slight cold sweats. The time for our departure couldn't have come at a better or worse time no matter how I looked at it.

I was about to say something to Graham in the context of my willingness to protect him when the lights flickered a few times then went off for about thirty seconds. The room went from being sufficiently lit, to complete darkness. The outside offered no help as the outside lights went out as well. I clenched Graham's arm, feeling his muscles tense at the same instance. We both shot up from where we were sitting. In my hesitation to let go of him, I stumbled over to the window to get a look though unfortunately I never had much of a view to begin with. As usual, there wasn't anything but trees and brush in either direction. The lights came back on briefly for about thirty seconds during which we both appeared stunned and were listening out for whatever we could. There was some yelling in the distance by what seemed to be a few male voices. Since we were both locked in this room together the outside noise put us on alert as it was all we had to depend on for the time being.

Graham rushed to the other side of the room to grab the bag of medications when the door opened and Louise came in. She looked around, seeing Graham and I being the only ones in the room and motioned for us both to follow her. Once we were outside of the room, she closed the door and we took an immediate right turn to the end of a short hallway, through a door and down a stairwell. She double checked to make sure we had the keycards.

"Alright guys, this is it. Once we get to the door down here you will need the keycards to get out– they both should still work. You can use yours first Graham. Seanna you should use yours next to get into the garage area after you go outside, take a right and then head straight toward the garages like Mia told you." Louise instructed quickly.

"Got it." Graham said as we both followed behind Louise and occasionally paused to listen for any sign of trouble. We marched down two flights of stairs to the main level.

The lights went off again as we got to the exit door. From the hallway the only visible lights came from the emergency flood lights that were in the hallways beyond the doors of the stairwell, which only partially illuminated the small area we were in. Louise motioned for Graham to come up where he presented his keycard. "I see this works both ways." he said, referring to getting in and getting out of the buildings. "Louise, thank you." I said as I stood in front of her and then got behind Graham. I put one hand on the backside of his waist and the other on the bag which hung in the grip of Graham's hand.

"I pray you two make it there safely." She hesitated slightly before backing away from us and the door and stepped back a few paces to stand on the bottom stair. When the lights flickered back on again signaling the electricity was on again, Graham swiped the keycard. The door handle twisted freely as he cracked the door open, checking nearby us for any movement. The darkness offered no help but it was possible to see the outline of the nearest building which was about seventy or eighty feet away. He crept outside as Louise immediately headed back upstairs. Before she made it halfway up the first flight, I spoke out to her quietly.

"Louise, where are you going to go now?"

She froze mid-flight, with her hand on the banister she turned around and replied in a loud whisper, "I'm going back to the desk area— I don't know you're gone yet!" Louise then turned and kept on up the stairs as I saw her body and feet disappear out of my view. Graham tugged at my arm which reminded me of our more difficult task ahead; getting to the garage undetected. Beyond that; an even more difficult and strenuous path. I peeked outside of the doorway for myself and saw the next building off in the distance.

Outside the air was humid and slightly warm— as if a good rain shower wasn't out of the question. I let the door close and we both moved to the corner edge of the building, Graham first as I diligently checked behind us to make sure no one was within view. He quickly leaned forward to get a quick glance and turned back to whisper to me that there were two security personnel walking along the perimeter of the grounds across from where we were. With the building layout being in a large diamond shape they would round one more building from the back way before approaching the one we just exited.

"They're walking pretty quickly— we gotta get around by the main building." Graham warned. I could sense the urgency and excitement in his voice.

"Get ready to stay low and close behind me." He added.

"I will— I'm ready." I whispered.

Graham nodded his head and looked around the corner again before he decided to cross the grassy area to get to the next building. While holding the bag in one hand he held out his other hand for me to take. I automatically grabbed it as he gave it a few quick squeezes— out of habit. I was plenty ready as he quickly took off with me, our feet only making minimal noise crunching against the blades of grass. Seconds later we rested ourselves against the next building with only the main building which sat far off to our right and the garage straight north from we were. The lights flickered again as the reflection of lights from off of the grass went off and then on.

My breaths had quickened while Graham remained almost entirely composed for the short run and burst of energy required to make it to where we were standing now. We continued close along the wall until we got to the corner that was closest to the garage and was it directly north in front of us. I could see the large building which up until now was in my mind as a much smaller unit. It didn't occur to me that the hundreds of people who traveled here may have needed to put their vehicles somewhere although I certainly didn't imagine a large open parking lot somewhere on the premises. The building was nearly two stories tall and just as big, if not bigger than the others. I looked behind us again to make sure that no one was following when I saw the back door of the building we just left being opened and two security guards quickly stepping outside. Their movements suggested that they knew I was missing from my room and the search was on. Again I could hear the buzz from their radio from where I was. Graham saw I wasn't right behind him and he quietly tried to get my attention. I rushed over to him.

"I think they know we're gone now." I whispered to Graham who was in front of me as we both crouched low at the corner edge waiting to cross in plain sight of any-one looking in our direction.

We both heard the chatter and buzz going on as radios flickered back and forth. From the windows above us, lights inside were being turned on which reflected onto the grass next to us.

"We have to keep moving, the garage is just over there beyond that brush." Gra-ham pointed with one hand as he held onto the straps of the bag with the other. He gave my right forearm a soft and quick squeeze which got my attention. I turned my head from looking back where we came from.

"Seanna, you okay?" He asked again

I nodded my head but said nothing. The fear was beginning to mount up inside. It was the kind of fear that put a solid knot in my throat. You'd think that of the many side effects of being infected, it'd be kind enough to remove the feeling of fear. If you asked me having the virus only exaggerates it.

"C'mon." Graham said as he took my hand and we ran for the patch of bushes and smaller trees that were near by the garage. It was about two hundred feet away and hard to see in the darkness but it was apparent that Graham had become familiar with the landscape during his week here. His helping out with building greenhouses and rooftop planters got him more exposure to the layout– which in turn would be helpful to us now. Graham ran much slower than he'd probably run on his own on account of my being bedridden for the last week. It felt like I was using some of the muscles in my legs for the first time. I used to run more often, for leisure and therefore out of habit I now automatically started pacing my breaths so they were more even.

The brush provided some cover though it was already inhabited by the bugs of the night. They weren't too happy about our intrusion and I had a quick thought to promise them we'd be out of their space as soon as we could. The buzzing and crawling of things I couldn't immediately see in the darkness has always been hard to ignore–especially when it came to moths which never flew in a straight line for longer than a nanosecond. From where we were, I could see behind us and somewhat see the space we just left because that area had more light nearby. The guards hadn't yet made it there though I was sure they'd come around the corner at any moment. We were now just one paved road across from the garage which had a large, commercial-sized automatic door that was much like the smaller ones used in home garages, this door however was wide enough for two cars at once. I could see the steel door entry way that the foot traffic used and was right off to the side of the driveway. Graham handed the bag over to me.

"Here, hold this– I have an idea." Graham said as he peered over to the garage and then over past me back toward the other buildings.

"What are you gonna do?" I was hoping it wasn't too dangerous.

He turned to face me, seemingly unaffected by the humming of the insects closest to us. I, on the other hand, was probably more annoyed than usual, swatting and cursing under my breath. Being nervous, full of fear and on the brink of more extraordinary pains at this point I'd probably be willing to do battle with whoever was on the other side of that garage door versus dealing with the insects.

"Baby, please don't go all Rambo on me." I said after it looked like he was figuring things out.

Aside from the seriousness of the moment he looked into my eyes and let out a chuckle. "Seanna, you are something else. No one but you would think of someone from a movie right now. Relax; I've gotten to know the guys that work in there pretty well. I think I can go and try the cardkey and if that doesn't work– I'll knock. When they answer, I'll just pretend I'm looking for you as well. Either way, I'll need to see who else is in there."

I started to shake my head in protest. It seemed too simple to work. What if they'd already been informed we both were gone? What if Davenport was already there waiting for us– making it to the garage before us while we were busy checking behind us to see if we were being followed? If they took Graham prisoner I would never leave him here alone to deal with my uncle and his police. No way.

"Babe, trust me. They weren't as concerned for me as they were for you. As far as they know, I'm in their little library looking up proper irrigating techniques." He said as he reached over and rested his hand on my arm. His confident touch– at least it felt confident to me spread the sense of control and certainty that he would be able to talk his way through most any situation waiting for him in that garage.

"Watch for the door opening. If it stays open for longer than a few seconds it means you can cross over and come in. I'll keep them distracted– just make sure you get over there." He whispered.

"Stay low and in the corner– you'll have plenty of cars to hide behind."

"Okay . . . Okay– please be careful, if you feel something's up– come right back. At this point I'm not above hopping the damn fence." I said as Graham acknowledged and crept out of the bushes. He looked back over past me before crossing the road which led to a dead end several yards from the garage driveway. Graham made it to the door, tried the card key— to no avail, all of which I could see from where I was in the bushes. I sighed and cursed again under my breath as Graham tried the card again multiple times, each of them denying entry inside. He turned to look at me and then further back behind me to see if anyone was coming toward the garage— which they still were not visible yet. He knocked just loud enough to where I could hear the echoes from the vibration of the door. Graham took another nervous glance off to the right side to where the road led to the main building. In the distance you could see a few flashlights which were maybe two hundred feet away. The road curved slightly but you could see three or four men assembled by the entrance. Becoming overwhelmed with worry now, I almost wanted to run over to where Graham was. Realizing it could possibly draw the attention of those looking for me I decided to stay where I was.

Graham quietly knocked a few more times before the door opened slightly. I could hear Graham's excited greeting to the man who opened the door and after a few seconds of dialogue, Graham was able to go into the doorway. With his back turned to me I could not hear his exact words— only that he was wondering if they heard on their radios or by phone— that I was missing and that he was helping to search for me. I did hear a response in the form of, 'Hey, man— sure come on in . . . When did they last see her?' before Graham disappeared inside and the door closed behind him.

The momentary silence almost drove me crazy. I could now just barely hear the voices of men at the building we just left. They were loud enough that my heart now moved up to my neck. I looked back one more time to see the men come around the corner quickly using flashlights to search any hidden areas. The moved around to the corner nearest to where I was and continued around the perimeter of the outside walls. I muttered under my breath, looking for the slightest light of the door to the garage being cracked open. Any little light would've sent me running across that road. I then started to think about what I would do if Graham never got the opportunity to open the door. I needed more than just a few large bushes to hide out in which were an obvious place to look for me before they searched the garage. I would guess about twenty more seconds passed with myself huddled alone in that grass before my legs just started moving. I quickly looked behind me to see the flashlights grouped together at the edge of the building we just left. I didn't know for sure at that moment but I assumed they would be on their way to check the garage next. My guess is they'd also check each and every room in every building if they had to. I stopped just short of the standard sized entry door that was made of reinforced steel and had only a small eyehole in addition to the knob. I ran to the side of the building and while using the walls as cover, waited for the door to open.

From where I was standing it appeared as if the men off in the distance were staying where they were— I saw no forward movements of their flashlights. I could feel pain building up at the middle of my torso which was about the same time my left arm and shoulder began to react and radiate in pain.

"Not now, not now." Was all I could murmur as I crouched down and began to take deep breaths. It had only been an hour tops since I got my last dose but I then assumed that was why they always gave me something for the pain along with it—which I haven't had all day. Little drops of perspiration began to form on my forehead as I held my sides and tried looking around the corner from an almost seated position. There was almost complete silence and no light peeking through the doorway so I turned back and began to focus on my breathing. I promised myself I would resolve the issue of pain as soon as I had the opportunity.

CHAPTER THIRTEEN

Sooner than I probably thought it took to go away, I opened my eyes a few seconds later after feeling some of the debilitating pain subside. It made me even more impatient and I wanted badly now to deviate from Graham's plan to wait for him to open the door for me to go in unnoticed. Perhaps I would go up to the door, knock and wait for whoever was assigned to the garage to open the door a little and I'd just bust in- forcefully taking one of the cars to get us to the Princeton lab. I let out a sigh of frustration and as if it were magic, the steel door opened a tiny crack. I waited a second as it did not close back, nor did anyone come out so I knew it had to be my cue to go inside. I scooped up the bag and scrambled to my feet, ignoring any residual pains that were left in me. Using both arms to get up, which I probably should not have done, was all in hindsight as I rushed to the door- carefully peeking through the crack before going in.

I could hear Graham's voice talking more than anyone else's as I checked around me one final time before going in. I pushed the heavy duty door open only wide enough as I needed to get in. I noticed there was a secondary heavy duty lock to match and I reached up and pushed it through in an attempt to ensure no surprise visitors from the outside. Following the plan, I hid myself behind a one of the cars, a sedan parked closest to the corner. Graham wasn't joking- there must've been a hundred cars parked in this garage. All of them were varying in models, colors and sizes as they belonged to the many Next Gen Tech Lab employees who reported in for work as usual or later traveled here in a panic with their families because of the distance and safety from the chaotic danger and mania going on within the bigger city limits. It was here where I would wait for any clue from Graham that it would be okay to come out.

"Yeah I don't see any sign of her in the building. Any vehicle keys would be in the office and no one's been in there 'cept the two of us. I don't know what else to tell you, Graham." I heard an unfamiliar male voice say. I peeked up out of curiosity, straining my neck to see who all was in the garage. There were two men aside from Graham who walked quickly but cautiously to get a look at each of the vehicles in all of the five rows. Though they had their backs to me, the one who spoke was slightly shorter and smaller than Graham. He wore a navy blue mechanics jumpsuit and tan work boots. The other man with them wore the same thing, was close to three inches taller than Graham and looked to be about forty pounds heavier.

"We should check the office and make sure none of the keys are missing, you think?" Graham suggested as the three of them continued along the walkway that was in between the second and last row of cars nearest to the wall where I was. They walked on a path that was marked in yellow paint similar to the parking spaces. They turned once they were halfway to the other end of the garage, presumably into the office area. It was about seventy-five feet from where I was but it was easy to see the light that came through the office window that looked out into the garage space. Even with the slight echo from the height of the garage, I could no longer hear any of the conversation when they went into the office so I was again forced to wait. I looked to the other sides of the garage and took in the layout. The direction Graham and the others went in spanned at least two hundred feet while the width was at least a hundred feet on its own. The inside was equally as humid as the outside as I looked up and saw large commercial fans slowly turning, quietly circulating the dense air.

Along several spots on the walls for convenience there were basic, older telephones. They became noticeable as they rang and echoed back and forth from each of their locations. The volume was loud and made my heart stop momentarily thinking about the caller and the subject matter to be disclosed to whomever answered. It would be no surprise at this point if the broadcast would be made that Graham and I are no longer accounted for– that we were missing. Whoever it was on the line could be calling to put the warning out to call security if we were seen. The phone was midway through its fourth ring before it was picked up. Sensing I couldn't be of any help from where I was, I peeked around the corner of the sedan to double check that indeed everyone who was in the garage was now in the office. I grabbed the bag and began to move closer to the office so I could get a better view as well as listen in. I stayed low and on the back row of cars before coming to the wall that would be the office on the inside. I could hear the same man's voice from earlier now talking on the phone.

"I understand the urgency. Like I said he's standing right here but the woman's not– he's looking for her too . . . I don't know how he knew she was missing, I just answered the door a few minutes ago and it was only him outside . . . You can ask him all that yourself– he'll tell better than I can . . . Okay, I guess not."

I heard a sound indicating the phone being hung up. From where I was hiding I could see the taller man now standing in the doorway looking out into the parked cars. He reached in his shirt pocket and pulled out a pack of cigarettes. He slowly scanned the area as he pulled one cigarette out, placed the pack back in his pocket and lit the cigarette without looking away from the cars. It wasn't hard to tell that he was thinking while surveying the modestly lit space. I quietly ducked back down to be sure I was well out of the man's line of sight as I heard the same guy on the phone now talking to Graham.

"They want us all to stay put. They'll be here in a few minutes." the man said, sounding frustrated.

"Alec, you know I wouldn't bother you all unless it was absolutely necessary. You guys are good guys, which is why I'm not happy to do this at all." Graham spoke regrettably.

"Whoa, whoa whoa! Dude he's got a gun!"

I heard the man named Alec say as my eyes widened and my head poked out from around the corner in shock. With the bag in hand, I immediately and dashed to the minivan in the next row. The tall guy still stood in the doorway but was now turned around, facing the inside office. His cigarette was still in his mouth but both hands were now slightly raised. It looked as if he was going to try to take off running but Graham quickly saw this and instructed him to step inside. I couldn't see the gun from where I was standing but I could see half of Graham from the window. He was calm, much calmer than I would be holding a gun and furthermore, pointing it at someone. Both of the men moved closer together as Graham maneuvered past them so he could be by the door.

"Seanna and I are leaving so none of this really concerns you, we just need a car, one with plenty of gas and we'll be on our way. Gentlemen, take a seat." Graham said after he took a deep breath. As the men were sitting down I quickly walked up to the doorway of the office. I announced myself to Graham which surprised both of the men. I sat the bag down by the doorway and stepped into the small office area which could accommodate three people at an "L" shaped desk. There was one computer, three smaller video monitors, a phone and a set of two-way radios that sat on the mostly tidy tabletop. I quickly glanced at the back wall that had a tall, portable metal utility closet and more importantly a section of what looked to be about one hundred numbered knobs that each held a set of keys for the cars parked outside of the office. It was exactly as described. I quickly turned my attentions back to my boyfriend who couldn't be more convincing to Alec and Joel- the name of the other man in the chair according to the name patch on his jumpsuit.

"Graham, baby do you think all of this is necessary?" I said, referring to his use of deadly force.

"Your girl's right man, I thought we were cool." Joel said.

"We're still cool. If you guys are held at gunpoint- it won't be your fault. Alec, look in that bottom drawer there and get the duct tape- very slowly of course," Graham instructed.

"*Very slowly.*" Alec mimicked but obliged him while muttering something under his breath and turned slowly to open the drawer.

"Dude, you know those guys have way more firepower than your one gun and they are gonna come down on you, hard once they get in here-.." Joel said. He looked at me in a way that suggested he'd be satisfied with that outcome.

"I put the lock on the front door," I said to Graham, as a matter of fact.

"They'll just blow it off." Joel added.

"The back door is locked too." Graham said.

Alec retrieved a full roll of duct tape from the drawer, closed it back and slowly turned so Graham could see that he had it in his hands. Graham instructed me to bind their hands and feet and warned them that if they made any noise that I'd tape their mouths as well. It wasn't easy for me to tie someone up– even though I knew it had to happen in order for us to get out of there unopposed. Graham again told them to behave as I started with Joel, taping his feet, winding in a circular motion around and around– seven or eight times each before moving up to bound their wrists. I figured it would be more effective if I bound their hands behind their back as they grumbled and swore under their breaths. I apologized, saying that they could get back to their jobs as soon as we left.

Alec and Joel now sat there somewhat awkwardly leaning forward a little as Graham helped to move them to the floor. I told them that at least they'd be little more out of the line of fire should things come to that. I was hoping that it wouldn't go that far. Graham tested the durability of the tape and seemingly satisfied with it, he gave me a nod. He told me to watch them as he went outside and jogged past the window– headed in the direction of the door we came in. To say the office was uncomfortable with him gone and Joel and Alec glaring at me– was an understatement. I didn't give them any eye contact as I instead walked to the door to see what Graham was up to. Graham was already jogging back to the office door where he stepped back inside.

"We should be alright for a while. Those doors are designed to keep people out." He reassured me.

"I hope you're right." I replied, nervously.

At the very same moment, we all heard vibrations coming from the door. We could also hear someone on the other side yelling, instructing someone to open the door. Graham didn't budge an inch as we stood there and listened until it stopped. His fingers deliberately checked the safety of the handgun as he carefully laid it on the desk next to the monitors. I couldn't help but stare at the manufacturer's emblem on the black polymer handle grip which was also printed out, Smith & Wesson along the stainless steel barrel. Graham flipped on the switch to all of the monitors and their screens turned blue in color. Someone outside banged on the door again a few times.

"Can you tell us why they're obviously pissed over you leaving? We deserve that much." Joel questioned.

Graham ignored Joel as he waited for a command screen to come up on the computer.

"Dude– come on, we're tied up– can we at least know why?" Joel exhaled, frustrated.

I looked at them both, pitifully sitting on the floor. They had nothing to do with what we were doing there. If I were in their shoes I'd want to know what was going on as well- and be reassured that my life wouldn't be taken for granted. As if on cue- the phone rang, which made us all jump. I knew it would be the next thing they'd try if no one answered the door. I also assume that the phone call is the step before they literally blow the door off from its hinges like Joel said a moment ago.

Graham was about to answer when I reached before him to answer. "I'll deal with this." I said as I picked up the phone and without anything quick-witted to recite, I calmly said, "Hello." There was about a five second pause before a voice that I was familiar with, one who also brought fear to me responded.

"I'll take my one-hundred dollars, as soon as this is over."

"What?"

It took me about five seconds to realize that Davenport wasn't talking to me. He was instead talking to someone next to him. It was equally confusing to Graham, Joel and Alec who all looked to me waiting to find out the tone of the situation at hand. I shrugged my shoulders indicating I had no clue either.

"It won't be long, isn't that right, Seanna?"

"You tell me." I replied.

Davenport while being aggressive was also the king of cool- along with the king of arms. I knew this was sort of a showdown and although it was true we had only one gun, I wasn't about to let him ruffle me. He would use his voice, authority and tactical knowledge to wear me into submission but I would use my own voice and the fact that I had nothing to lose anymore to keep everything level. My mission was the same. I could tell the virus inside of me picked the perfect time to act up again. I could feel pain again coming on. I moved the phone away from my face to take a deep breath, holding my hand up to Graham who was ready to take the phone on my behalf. I put it back to my ear and sat on the desk while Davenport began his attempt to break me down.

"Okay, I'll take a stab at it. Your desire is to get off of the premises . . . A wild guess says you'd use one of those cars inside to head somewhere in the direction of, ah, Princeton, perhaps."

My mouth dropped as my eyes widened and searched the floor for answers. I tried not to say anything or respond as Graham waited anxiously. He put his hand on my leg which got my attention. I pointed at a pen that was on the desk a few feet away. Graham handed it to me along with a piece of paper from the top of a stack in the corner. I neatly scribbled, 'He knows' on the corner, large enough for Graham to see.

"Your uncle knows?" Graham whispered to me. I shook my head, missing part of Davenport's rambling.

" . . . told you before of your options. The reality is that you are confined to a space that's surrounded and it will be only a short time before those doors go down and you and your boyfriend go down as well."

"Your point, Mr. Davenport?" I said, trying not to skip or stutter my words.

"Dr. Burges and Dr. Strauss will be here shortly. I would hope not to have your uncle see things go a certain way but I will have this resolved, at whatever end, short-ly."

"Good, you can tell him to call me when he gets here." I replied as I hung up and took a deep breath.

I felt my point was made and although hanging up on him was a decision made in haste, I hoped that Davenport would wait until my uncle made it to the garage before barging in and taking us down as he described. I figure I bought us a few minutes to get our game plan together. I told Graham what Davenport told me and while Joel and Alec sighed and whined about our doom– theirs included. I told Graham it was time to get our act together so we could make a decent attempt to get as far as we could. When he figured it was Davenport I had talked to, he lost none of his spirit– which I was glad, because Davenport had certainly put fear into me over the last week. He liked to pull triggers and I was already familiar with that quality in him.

Graham ran his fingers through his hair and I naturally went closer by his side, standing near him as he quickly worked through his mind a plan of action. I rested my arm on his shoulder and tried on my own to think up the best solution possible.

"They know about Princeton . . . " I reiterated.

"It doesn't change the fact we need to get out of here," he said as he put his hand on my arm and gave it a squeeze.

Graham looked over at the keys on the wall.

"The yellow knobs are the keys to the armed trucks right?" He asked Joel.

"Yeah, but there are no weapons in them– they take 'em out every time they park 'em."

"Good."

Graham got up, took the gun from off the desk and went to the wall where the keys were. He grabbed two sets under the yellow numbered knob labeled 'two' and 'three'. He told us to sit tight while he ran out of the office again. Thirty seconds later I could hear the door of a vehicle opening followed the sound of a diesel engine roar to life as it switched gear, accelerated– moving for a little while and then was put back in park and then turned off. I went to the doorway of the office in time to see that he parked the van sideways next to the back entrance door of the garage. Graham was now in the second armored van– come to think of it, which was probably among the same vans that were at his house and brought us here. He turned the engine on and this time drove past the office where I stood toward the front of the garage and man-euvered the vehicle to block the door through which we came. He climbed out of the vehicle and started jogging toward the garage again.

The phone rang.

I quickly went to answer it and sat in the chair where Graham sat before. I picked up the phone but said nothing this time. I didn't know who or what to expect. My face and arms began to sweat as I automatically wiped my forehead and looked over in time to see Graham back in the doorway.

"Seanna . . . . Seanna, are you on the line?"

"Yes."

I heard a heavy exhale before my uncle Lloyd started talking again.

"Sweetheart, you're the cause of a lot of concern right now. How are you feeling?"

There was a long pause before I decided to speak.

"I'm taking Graham and we are leaving- simple as that. You can tell your pitbull Davenport to back off and let us go."

There was a long pause before Lloyd decided to speak.

"Seanna, I can't let you do that . . . I think you understand in your heart and mind, why."

"You know Uncle, I knew you'd say that but I don't understand. We talked about my will before in your office. I still have my will- but you won't honor it. Since I was brought here I'm remembering some things from my childhood that I didn't before. I remember my mother taking my brother and I to what I thought was the doctor's office for check-ups. I sense now that something from that time is connected to what's going on now." I recalled.

"Your mother wasn't ever fond of lying, Seanna. Did she ever explain to you her troubles conceiving after her and my brother married?"

During the pause, I could hear several voices in the background but no clear dialogue.

"No, she did not."

As far as I knew I was born four years after they were married in the summer of eighty-five. The fact that I was born in eighty-nine wasn't an exceptional scenario. I figured my mother wanted to explore her career options a little while after graduating from Rutgers. That along with her newly immigrated husband, my father who I'm sure wanted to take some time to get used to living here in America and settling down to find a job. It made perfect sense to me and sounded responsible, in all honesty.

"Well my dear you might've been born earlier if they had their wish. They wanted to start a family right away."

Again, I said nothing.

"Your mother and father came to me after two years of trying- hoping to experience the blessing of childbirth. They were both aware of recent accomplishments with in-vitro fertilization and as a young doctor, I was eager to help . . . You're here as a result of those efforts, so is your brother. Though it was unconventional it was possible, nonetheless."

They had been successfully creating families in the laboratory since the late seventies- which was okay with me. I was glad I was here. It was only a slight shock for me right now and probably made for more juicy gossip to someone else. I wanted to know what this had to do with what was going on right now.

"Okay, so my mother and father needed some help, what does this have to do with it now?"

"Besides her husband, your mother wanted to have you and your brother more than anything else in the world. She would've done almost anything after almost two years of trying. Imagine, month after month of negative pregnancy tests. My brother's fertility tests were normal so the issue seemed to be her. She took this to heart- knowing the thousands of dollars it would've cost her for treatment after treatment with no guarantee. At the time it would've cost tens of thousands of dollars to successfully carry a baby to term- on their own."

"Yes. So where do you factor into all of this? Where does all of *this* and eighty-nine factor into all of it?" I said, referring to the facility we were now in.

"It's more like nineteen eighty-eight. You weren't conceived until late fall of that year, obviously. Before then there were tests done in the lab- the standards were newly set in the U.S. for those kinds of fertilization methods. At the same time there was a sort of curiosity growing for the extension of life at the cellular level. I don't have time to teach cellular biology as I know it- but I will suffice to say that a small, but highly influential group of scientists at that point were curious about cellular regen- eration now that we could create human life and sustain it in the lab. All we basically needed was X and Y."

I was beginning to be bothered by my uncle's description of what happened during that time. My parents never talked about that time in our family history so I figured it was never a big deal to begin with. I doubt that there are many other people out there who are that interested in how long it took for their parents to conceive children, esp- ecially when the oldest was born only four years after marriage. It all just seemed normal. I looked around at Joel and Alec who were both flustered, excited and tired- looking at the same time. Graham had disappeared again out into the garage area again before I knew it. Part of me secretly wanted to negotiate a deal to somehow ex- change everyone except me- to guarantee their safety while I would try and make it to Princeton on my own. Davenport just told me flat out that he was aware of our plans to go to the University laboratory. I loved Graham more than I could ever say but not enough to risk his life trying to get out of here. I weighed a lot in my mind while my uncle was telling me that my mother conceived me unnaturally at such a young age.

"Seanna, darling you need to know that it wasn't it as bad as you think. Your mother was able to carry you and junior to term."

"Okay, so what's the big deal, then?"

"The big deal is in stem cells. You know it's always been the promise land- even now for treatment of disease such as Parkinson's and spinal cord injuries. There's even the possibility to regenerate certain dead cells to an extent. Where there are cells, there are whole organisms." He said as his voice began to gain an excited but cautious tone.

"That's a little far-fetched don't you think?" I began to say before I was cut off.

"You and your brother's DNA, yours and his cells were a part of formula that was used for cellular regeneration projects. Honestly the technology was not entirely supportive of such endeavors until recently so your samples sat frozen for almost two decades. We used yours first because you were the oldest, of course."

I couldn't believe what was coming from his mouth. I knew where this was headed– I just didn't want to hear anymore.

"Something obviously got fucked up, uncle. We have dead people strolling around, if you haven't noticed. Please don't tell me this shithole of an experience that's affected millions of people is because of you." I said, trying to keep my composure.

"Not mine, directly. There's always someone willing to push the limits though– which is why I need you to stay here, Seanna. You are carrying an infection that, in you, is more like the blood of your relatives. You and it are coexisting in the same body and you're alive still– it's nothing short of amazing."

I don't know where my uncle's been the last week but the virus has not been 'co-existing' with me. I've constantly been on the brink of death and when I'm not briefly crossing over into deadness, I'm battling intermittent pains that at their peak could make a whale walk on land.

"You have an interesting interpretation of what it means to co-exist . . . Is that what you think we'll be able to do? Get this all under control and *co-exist* with it? If that's the case, you can send someone in to put a bullet in my head right now." I said truthfully.

"Seanna, that's not what it's about. I'm here going to these extents to correct someone else's mistake."

I heard another voice say something to my uncle. It sounded like they said, 'We're ready when you're ready'. I looked up at Graham who was now standing right next to me. I covered the mouthpiece of the phone as I whispered to him that they are about to try something. With his gun in hand, he immediately went to the door to look for any signs they were coming in. My uncle spoke to me once again.

"Seanna, if the screen on the computer monitor isn't already on– will you please turn it on? Any of the monitors will work, actually. We're patched into all of them."

The monitor Graham had turned on all of a sudden went from black with the NGT Labs logo to a blank grey screen and then quickly turned to a picture of a plain, sparsely furnished room in black and white video. I didn't need to have a color picture to see there were two people there– a male and a female. My eyesight registered their identities quicker than my mind could process, or it could have been shock setting in as a buffer but I saw countless experiences with them flash in front of me, almost as if I were dying. It was already too late for my mother and my father.

"Oh *shit*, is that your– . . . ?" Graham started to say, leaning in to get a closer look at the screen.

It was both of them, except that they were no longer breathing or able to smile, talk or sadly be my living parents. I saw their listless faces and bodies shuffling slowly around the room. They were pale even by the standards of the black and white video feed. My mother Ivy wore a button up, long sleeve shirt that looked like it had a large smear of blood on its sleeve. It was the shirt she always wore when she did housework as it was too big on her but she found it was comfortable. Her hair was only slightly out of place, in a loose ponytail, and partially gray as I remembered it from

Easter when we all had dinner together. My father was dressed in jeans and dark polo shirt– something that tells me they both were able to be off from work that day, whenever they got infected. The video feed was slightly grainy but I could tell from the way they walked around the room they no longer acknowledged each other; instead they only paced around the medium sized room that lacked any furniture with the exception of a single bed and a chair that was turned over on its side. I took all of this in within a matter of seconds. I could feel Graham's hand giving my shoulder a squeeze, however I sat there– frozen, almost forgetting the phone was up to my ear.

"I'm so sorry, my niece . . . Sorry you had to see them like this. You wouldn't believe me if I only told you. This is why– they are why I need you here with us." Lloyd spoke solemnly.

My eye's blurred as the tears begin to stream down my face. I could feel my face flush with warmth as I began to wipe the moisture from my eyes. I couldn't take my eyes from off of the screen, Emotionally, I was trapped I couldn't yell out, though I wanted to– I couldn't speak. I hoped this was some demented joke my uncle and NGT– hell, even my parents were pulling just to get me to stay.

I could hear Joel and Alec behind me but I couldn't move from the spot I was in.

"Dude, I think those are her parents," Alec whispered to Joel from where they were seated a few feet away.

There was silence on both ends of the phone for almost a minute before Lloyd spoke again. Graham just kept patting my back softly, in a circular motion.

"Your mother truly loved my brother . . . They were both infected by the time they came here. Jackson was worse off and clearly was going to go first. She never left his side. They both wanted to be together even after passing so we honored their request and kept them in the same room."

I couldn't listen to anymore, so I just hung up. I wanted to tell him something witty or tell him to rot in hell but it wouldn't do justice. As soon as the phone was disconnected Graham practically picked me up by the shoulders and gave me a long and hard hug. He whispered, "I'm sorry, I wanted them to be okay too." I began to sob in his arms as the phone rang again. Neither of us moved.

CHAPTER FOURTEEN

"He said they were infected when they got here." I cried into Graham's shoulder while the phone kept ringing. I took a big sniffle and wiped my nose with my sleeve.

Holding on to hope for anything good was becoming increasingly difficult at an exponential rate. I slumped back down into the chair as Graham helped to guide me into the seat. I buried my face into my hands. I didn't immediately see him reach past me nor did I object to his turning the computer monitor off which still broadcast the live video feed of my parents' staggering. No one, including myself, needed to see my parents deceased, wandering around– especially now they've become the most hated and feared group on the planet. I didn't know exactly how long it'd been since they'd joined the masses which were now a direct threat to the survival and future of mankind.

"If you want to go back now, I understand– I'll even go back with you." I said through the palms of my hands.

Graham did not rush to respond. It was as if he waited for the annoying tone of the phone ringing to stop which was only a few seconds later. He pulled up the second office chair and sat right in front of me. He took my hands down from my face, disregarding my potentially virus-saturated tears. "I'm not worried about what's outside." he calmly said as he held my hands and looked into my eyes. His brownish-green eyes were frequently able to catch my attention for any little thing he wanted me for. Usually it was for some non-critical or even romantically playful tidbit but today apparently it was for a serious pep- talk.

"Babe, I can't even begin to put myself in your shoes right now . . . To find out like this . . . I'm sorry about your mom and dad. They were good people. They loved each other and they loved you. I don't know how they felt about this place but I know they'd want you to have the best chance to live– especially now that they can't . . . I'm not going back, neither should you. Our plan should remain the same."

Reflecting on his thoughtful and heartfelt guidance, I took it seriously– remembering all I knew about his deceased parents who departed when he was seventeen, suddenly in a boating accident. He was not present when it happened and yet similarly, he experienced the same sort of instant, tragic loss that I now was forced to absorb. As of now, he and I had another connection, an unfortunate similaritybvgbn which made me uneasy. Though I saw death frequently on the job, a person in my career learns quickly to build a buffer– a way to prevent you from taking your job home with you. All the faces you see that were sometimes lifeless, at other times in shock or pain – either way, in need of your services, the crying and moaning , the smell and sight of blood. Nothing can prepare you for seeing your loved ones in that same manner.

"I don't want to lose you too, here or out there. It's bad enough my parents are now dead . . . Maybe I haven't given my uncle and the lab here a chance." The tears began to fall again as soon as I said the words *parents* and *dead* in the same sentence. To see them so disconnected and unhuman even though they still resembled the people I loved and would've gladly traded my life for, a hundred times over was nothing I'd soon forget.

"We can always come back if things don't pan out over at Princeton– as you can see from all of this I'm pretty positive they won't turn you away." Graham said, bringing up a very valid point. Who says we have to stay anywhere for extended time? Last I checked I wasn't convicted of a crime and confined to any one spot for any length of time.

"Man, that is *so* sad," Joel said.

I looked over at him but said nothing.

"No seriously, that guy– your dad, he was a nice guy. It didn't seem like he was infected or anything when they came here. I checked in their car myself. I remember him from the other families because he wasn't an employee. He told us he was the brother of one of the guys in charge. He offered to come back and help us out with building and structural improvements– you know, to make sure things were safe around here." Joel added.

That was exactly the kind of man my father was. Though he was often thought of as introverted to people who didn't know him, he was always willing to be helpful whenever he could pitch in. To know they drove here, probably in an absolute panic, wore down my heart and reiterated the untimely end they came to.

"We keep going." I confirmed, simple as that.

"Let's do it, then." Graham said as he patted my leg and got up to walk toward the wall where the keys to all of the vehicles in the garage hung. He started naming off the makes of cars according to what he saw on the key rings. "We have Honda, Chevy, Acura, Pontiac, oooh Mercedes– . . . "

"We're taking the Caddy." I replied, referring to my uncle Lloyd's Cadillac CTS-V. If I remembered correctly, he owned the newest model year. It was a brief topic of conversation this past fall when he replaced his three year old CTS, affirming that business was good in regards to his career at NGT.

Graham by now was easily able to confirm with Joel its place on the number one knob where the keys hung was in fact Lloyd's car- that, along with the visible multi-colored Cadillac emblem on the keys and keyless remote. He took the keys down from the knob and after pausing for thought, grabbed three additional set of keys from the knobs nearby.

"For the diversion." Graham said as he marched back around Joel, Alec and my chair on his way out of the office door. I got up to follow him but was immediately struck down by a surge of pain which instantly brought on cold sweats. The phone began to ring for the third time, which met the end of both my patience and kindness. After pausing to deal with the sudden onset of pain, before I knew it I answered the phone with a curt, "Will you give us a minute?" and hung the phone back up while Davenport was in mid-sentence. I buried my face back into my hands, sitting there waiting for the intensity to settle down before I remembered the black bag by the doorway. While I waited, the tears began to fall, yet again as I reverted back to the thoughts and memories of my mom and dad. The pains that I have been feeling- they must have felt too. I could picture my mother attempting to comfort my father as he went through the painful attacks repeatedly. I knew of these all too well. My mother would endure the same, perhaps on her own in the end with my father too far gone in a coma.

As soon as I was able, I went directly to the bag to get a syringe of the anti-viral along with some pain pills that were likely Percocet. I clutched them both tightly in my hand as I saw Graham drive by in one of the sedans. I peeked out of the doorway in time to see him park it close to the extra wide garage door. He got out and jogged to another car nearby the door where with the keys in hand, started the engine and parked it too, next to the first sedan. He did this a third time with a pickup truck before he jogged back to the office where he grabbed the bag and my hand as soon as he saw the syringes out.

"I'm guessing you need a minute to take those while I figure out how to get us both in the car and that garage door open- without getting shot."

"I don't want to take this and be out of it- not right now. It hasn't even been three hours yet, the pain just came out of nowhere." I said. Confident I might regret doing so, I placed the syringe and pills in my zip pocket for later- praying there was a later.

"We can help you both and open the door, if you'll un-tape us," Joel interrupted.

"It'll be in your best interest if you and Alec stay out of it." Graham insisted.

"Look, the remote button to open the garage is right there on wall- if you open it now you can forget about getting to the car in time or getting out of here. I'm sure they're blocking the exit from the other side but you won't see how blocked it is until the door is open. Bottom line, you need our help." Alec argued.

Alec was especially irritated by the whole incident. I was too. They were right but it was impossible to tell if they were trustworthy. For all I knew they probably had another gun somewhere as I would expect them to be armed. The two of them could be simply waiting for an opportunity to get to it and flip things around. I figure it was a scenario my uncle would be the happiest with. Davenport could just come right in, ruin our plans and probably kill Graham just to make a point. I started questioning Joel because if we were to release either of them– it would be him.

"How do we know we can trust you Joel? It'd be too easy to just grab the weapon they designated to keep in this area in case of an attack and use it against us. I want to trust you." I said as the pain was starting to wear off on its own. This made it much easier to plead my case to him. I decided I would speak first, instead.

"Without telling you too much, I'll tell you that we don't have anything that belongs to NGT so they have no right to keep us here against our will– no right at all. It's bad enough my parents are now dead and I know for a fact that I'll die here too if I stay any longer." I continued, wiping sweat from my brow. Graham saw the distress I was experiencing and stood by my side, rubbing my back.

Joel lowered his head for a moment, to think.

"There's another gun– loaded, right inside where the fire blanket box is, over there. If I didn't want to help I wouldn't have told you that. The quicker you guys try and get out of here the sooner we'll be out of harm's way. I figure you guys have your reasons for wanting out– whatever they are– that's your business." Joel said. Alec nodded too in agreement as Graham rushed over to the fire blanket box that was right by the entrance to the office. He opened the lid to the red box with the highly visible white letters. Inside was an all black, semi– automatic handgun with a spare magazine clip.

"Can you handle this?" Graham said, handing it to me after looking the pistol over and checking that the safety was on. I said nothing as I nodded and accepted the fire–arm– which was generally heavier than I remembered they were. I'd fired a handgun on a few occasions out of curiosity after going to the range in Allentown. When I first moved out on my own, I contemplated purchasing one for home defense. I ultimately decided against it because of my future occupation and the fact that I was going into the field of preserving life. It also helped that I moved into the second floor of a medium sized apartment complex versus a ground level so I figured my odds were pretty good against home invasion.

I held the gun in my hands, switching the safety off and on again– squeezing the pistol grip while trying to recall everything I learned about firearm mechanics and safety during my visits to the range years ago. The gun was a thirty-two caliber, smaller than Graham's forty caliber but effective nonetheless against a dead one or anyone with a well-aimed shot to the head. If I remember correctly it was recom-mended to me as a first timer's alternative to the thirty–eight revolver.

My goal was not to be intimidating so I placed the gun on the desktop behind me. Joel was right, he didn't have to mention the pistol so it was now my turn to give him the benefit of the doubt.

"We need to get going. I trust you want us out of here so I will cut you lose." I said as I looked around for scissors which happened to be laying flat in the corner by the wall. I started to cut Joel free, beginning with his legs, when the phone began to ring–yet again. Instead of answering it Graham went to the office doorway and looked in both directions. I apologized to both Joel and Alec who by now understood that only

Joel would go free. I told Alec to sit tight— he would be freed as soon as we got out of there. Once Joel was unbound I returned to the desk and scooped up the gun, making sure Joel could see I was in possession of it. He seemed unfazed by my gesture; instead he went to look out through the office window onto the vehicles— perhaps more interested in what Graham had done the last few minutes.

"I was gonna turn on the brights, maybe try and blind 'em," Graham said to Joel.

"Yeah, I would say have the engines running too— just so they can't tell which one you're in." Joel agreed.

They both nodded at each other. Graham being a gentleman, extended his hand to shake with Joel's. Joel reluctant at first, obliged and said there were no hard feelings. He glanced at us both and said he hoped we'd make it to our destination. It was my turn to apologize and thank Joel and Alec as I gave them a quick nod. I grabbed Graham's hand with one and the black bag with the other as I followed behind him out of the office door. Joel followed behind us as he said he'd wait until all the engines were on and we were safely in the car before he'd flip the switch to let the door up. In the growing distance between the office and where we were going, I looked back as I heard the phones around us ring in unison. Graham led us to the number one parking spot. Awaiting us was a two- door, metallic black Cadillac coupe that even its grungy confines, looked like it fell out of a magazine advertisement. From our side approach, the slightly tinted windows revealed an equally dark interior. The car lit up slightly as Graham hit the keyless entry button and let go of my hand. On a normal occasion, even the slightest car enthusiast would take note of the pristine exterior and even more, sleek and cozy high-tech interior such as the Recaro leather seats. Neither of us took much longer to admire the vehicle as we both slid in, closed the doors and Graham started the car. I tried to sit as comfortably as I could with a gun at my side and with no luck I slid the gun into the pocket of my hooded jacket. I sat the black bag on the floor mat of the backseat behind me. We sped past the office where we saw Joel standing, acknowledging us from the doorway. Graham pulled alongside the pickup truck on the end which by now formed a semi circle where he hopped out to start the engines of the other cars. He started with the sedan lined up on the opposite end. I could see him from where I was, fumbling a little to adjust the headlight settings to their brightest before he got out, closed the door and went to the next car to do the same. I refused to just sit there while he did all of the work so I got out and headed for the pickup truck to follow. I could see Graham's disapproval when he saw I was out of the car. I'd welcome the discussion about it later, when we were somewhere safe.

I stumbled a little but beat him to the pickup truck where he shook his head and mumbled, "You just won't sit still— will you?"

"No, sir." I replied as I turned the engine on. The pickup hesitated but turned over on the second try where then I searched the dash and steering column for the switch to turn on the bright lights. Graham was leaning in to help but we both heard yelling coming from the direction of the office. Both of us looked in time to see Joel in the doorway with his hands cuffed around his mouth yelling for us.

"Hurry– they're coming in!" Joel repeated twice before we understood.

The side door that we came through, the one I managed to put the bolt lock on, started to vibrate forcefully with loud, repeated thuds. The metal on the door was thick, most likely steel reinforced which made it heavy but it was very possible that at any second the lock would give. The vehicles parked in front of the door would provide a little extra time. Graham extended his hand to me as I scrambled to get out of the car. We both took off to get back to the Cadillac that thankfully, Graham left running. He yelled back to Joel for the go-ahead before closing the car door and turning on our own headlight setting to bright and putting the car in drive. Although the inside of the car was well insulated from outside noise, the vibration could be felt from where we were. It stopped however, at the same time the garage door lifted, slowly exposing our view to the outside. I saw at least two pairs of black boots scramble across the wide entryway as the door lifted up to knee level before they were out of view.

The bright lights must've temporarily confused everyone on the outside because by the time the door raised completely– all movement ceased. With the exception of one of the heavy duty pickup trucks parked along the side of the road, the area was cleared in all directions across to the tiny service road to the brush where Graham and I hid earlier. It was intensely lit up now from all the vehicle lights. We both ducked down as far as we could in an attempt to not be seen while the Cadillac's engine hummed, ever so slightly.

What seemed like minutes only amounted to seconds before the end of a long assault rifle poked out from the edge of the garage entry. Presumably, one of Davenport's armed men, dressed in black protective gear crept low and slowly approached the first sedan Graham parked. If he started on the opposite side we would've had to flee immediately. As if it made a difference Graham and I stayed absolutely still. I watched as the man pointed the automatic rifle at the car and walked around the vehicle quickly inspecting it.

"Graham we should go!" I whispered as if they could possibly hear us from outside.

"Not yet, someone has to be covering him." he calmly replied.

The armed man, seemingly confident the car was empty, turned around and focused on the second sedan next to it. He threw up a few hand signals which prompted the movements of four more men; two emerged from the same side he came from and two appeared right at the side where we were waiting. They might've seen us immediately– I could see their heads but it was Joel who sparked their attention next. Neither Graham nor I could hear anything Joel said but assumingly it was more than enough to divert their attentions for the few seconds we needed.

I heard Graham calmly tell me to hold on as he shifted the luxury sedan to drive and as expected, the horsepower and acceleration caused my hands to clench both sides of the seat and pushed my back into the seat with impressive force. Before I could blink, Graham had pressed down on the gas pedal and sat up in time to see the immediate need to turn the car left onto the service road. The sway of the car forced my body again onto the door which thankfully locked on their own once the car moved forward. The surprised faces of the armed men were in the rear view as Graham yell-ed out, "They're gonna shoot!"

I shrieked once I heard them fire and the instantaneous impact of several bullets hit the body of the Cadillac as we sped at more than a safe speed toward the main building a few hundred yards down the road. I looked out of the back window in time to see a few bodies run to the pickup truck that was parked across the way. From my own seat I was able to see the headlights turn on immediately after.

"Shit, they're coming!" I yelled.

"Buckle up," Graham firmly suggested. His focus switched back and forth from the rear view mirror to the road ahead.

"You first," I said as I began to help him connect his buckle. I connected my own as the main building sank farther from our rear view. The road turned slightly to the left as our speed along with the total darkness yielded nothing but the shapes of tall trees and not much else. Graham adjusted the headlight setting back to normal. We made yet another slight left turn down the road as I looked back to see the headlights of the truck in the distance. I looked at the speedometer which read almost seventy briefly before we slowed to make a turn.

"Here comes the gate! Hold on!" Graham said.

I looked forward in time to see us rapidly approaching yet another utility truck blocking the exit and the gate. The gatehouse was maybe one hundred yards away with several bodies coming out. They also had guns. It was easy to tell from their confident strides and the way they readied themselves for our approach. They were quickly stepping out and preparing to aim when Graham slowed down suddenly and veered off of the road into an opening between the trees. Thankfully, the area was mostly flat. We both gasped for air simultaneously as he took to steering through the brush and knee high grass. The car rocked in response as we ran over various large branches and smaller bushes. The direction we were headed led us nearly to the fence, we were now close by. Had it not been for the need to clear a path for the newly resurrected chain link fence with barbed wire woven through the top, it would've been impossible to drive along side it. The limited visibility from the darkness caused Graham to slow down even more as he crept along the perimeter at times needing to steer out of the way of various debris and larger branches.

"We can't just bust through the fence . . . the airbags. The road is right on the other side– I can see it." Graham said.

I knew exactly what he meant about not busting through the gate head-on. Sooner or later we would also run into the end of this fence and have no choice but to go through it. I turned around in the seat once again to see if we were still being followed and was almost overjoyed by their absence until a second later when I saw the rock-ing motion and flicker of lights between the trees not too far behind. The truck too had most likely veered off at the same time to follow our exact path, winding and turning between the brush and trees.

I could see the anxiety building up in Graham too as he looked into the rear view mirror repeatedly, seeing the same things I did. The pickup truck was likely much more capable of handling the less than ideal surface this fancy coupe wasn't designed for because the distance between the two vehicles became shorter and shorter. Our bodies rocked side to side and back and forth as the wheels on the coupe struggled to maintain traction on the uneven surface that was littered with small branches, piles of grass and other debris from the fence construction. It seemed as if at any second, we'd get stuck. The sound of the tire rotation was obvious with the ample horsepower whenever Graham attempted to accelerate. Instead of increasing speed, the car only rocked more than before.

"To hell with it, hold on!" Graham warned. He looked left over his shoulder as if he were simply changing lanes in traffic.

He veered the sedan left, causing it to come into contact with the fence a few seconds later. The fence gave easily at first because the car was between two fence poles but more resistance followed right before we heard the bending of the metal poles connected to the chain link fence. We managed to catch the fence for a split second before rolling over all of it due to its remaining connected to the other sections. More important was the absence of the airbags which would've created more problems had they been deployed. Graham steered right and quickly met up with the highway that ran parallel to the property not more than a ten yards away. He immediately accelerated and the speedometer confirmed the increase to nearly eighty. I was frozen in my seat until we were well over the pavement where I yelled out an exuberant "*Yes, yes, go baby, go!*" to Graham who remained focused as we sped down the dark highway.

"Can you see them?" Graham asked when I turned around in my seat again to look for the headlights behind us.

"Yeah." I mumbled as I slumped back down into the seat.

The surrounding darkness was eerie and ominous. I felt tension build up in the pit of my stomach. We were finally on our way from NGT, my uncle and the unforgettably-pesky Davenport. It was a plan that was officially in the works for several days by at least several individuals.

As we sped down the two lane stretch of road we encountered quite a few abandoned vehicles that thankfully were parked along the shoulder. At our current speed it would be difficult to say whether or not we would have enough stopping distance should the need arise for us to break suddenly. I wished there was some way I could inform Mia, Dr. Chavan, Ruben and even Laura right now that Graham and I were off of the property and the plan worked in its own haphazard fashion. Though it was premature to declare a victory with the heavy duty pickup truck still in our rear view, nevertheless, a major step had been accomplished.

"We need to swing back around since we're now going the opposite direction from Princeton." Graham warned as we coincidentally sped past a sign that indicated we were on a county road headed south. "I think we should keep going in this direction," I replied, remembering my conversation with Davenport. He knew we were headed to the Princeton lab specifically. By Dr. Chavan supplying us with a week's worth of the anti-viral and pain killer it provided us with more than enough leeway to wait, a few days if necessary before attempting to head toward the University lab.

"Makes sense to me. We need to get far away from these menaces first and then find someplace to lay low for a few days- maybe try to get in touch with the Princeton lab on our own." Graham spoke while focusing on driving as safely as we could while at such a high rate of speed. Most of the time my head was turned to look out of the rear window but occasionally I glanced off to the side of the road. The darkness failed to provide many details, only that there was an occasional house or business- none of which would be safe enough for us to stop even if we weren't being pursued. For starters, they were too conveniently located. Second and more importantly, there were a couple bodies moving around. Dead-ones had descended upon these locations and for some reason they were rewarded enough to stick around. I looked out of the window in amazement at one of the buildings, a small grocery store as we sped past. There wasn't any electricity in the form of light but you could see several figures moving around slothfully, nearby an open entrance. It was plain to see the building had been invaded. Anyone hoping to avoid contact with a dead one appeared to be out of luck at this location.

My own adrenaline lowered again, enough for me to notice pains in my shoulder and arms starting to return. I surely didn't need Graham to worry about me now. I wanted him to keep us moving so we would hopefully lose the pickup truck. I closed my eyes, took a deep breath and lowered the passenger window to let in some fresh air. Of course, this caused Graham to become concerned and to make things worse, the air was humid and smelled like anything but fresh. There was no rotten stench or the smell of smoke like the television reports, earlier. This odor was woodsy, moist and almost thick enough to cut with a butter knife. Clearly in the time it was since we left the room at NGT the humidity had picked up quite a bit. I hit the button to close the window back up and quickly fumbled around the dashboard for the air conditioning.

"Don't worry about me, just keep driving." I said before Graham could begin to express concern. He knew me well enough to not take it personal. After all, both of our safety was way more important than mine on its own- especially when we were speeding and trying not to get wrapped around a tree. I strained to look back again and although our speed increased at times and decreased at others to make it safely around a turn, the pickup truck was able to maintain a reasonable proximity. The headlights were likely never more than a half of a mile from our rear view mirror.

In my best estimation we'd travelled a little more than nine miles from NGT. The landscape was beginning to change as the flatter plains began to give way to occasionally higher landscape. The road remained even but it was easy to see the increase in guard rails because of the increase in rivers and creeks that were to the sides below road we were on. In the daylight and sans the viral outbreak perhaps it would ordinarily be a scenic drive, beautiful and the road would be flush with avid campers and visitors from other states.

I thought we could continue like this forever, even with the vehicle perhaps carrying Davenport and his most skilled and trusted guys not too far behind us. With the laws of mathematics at a constant, any decrease in speed meant a decrease in the distance between us. Graham kept his foot on the gas and was cautiously alert however there was no chance of avoiding everything. We were cruising along, going about seventy-five around a slight curve- which this lovely Cadillac handled oh, so well. The sign suggested that traffic go no more than forty for the turn but it wouldn't have made a difference with the decision Graham had to make only a hundred feet away. In his defense, who in their right mind would put a road right there? Better yet, why would someone choose to travel at this time of night? Last I checked, it was close to one o'clock, a time when according to every news source, the dead ones were highly active. Whoever it was in the Buick we swiped at nearly seventy five miles an hour had to have a dire need to be on the road at that time, just like we did.

Maybe we weren't going seventy-five; perhaps it was only sixty by the time we hit them. It made no difference as Graham had all of two seconds to slow before we made impact with the sedan in the midst of making a right turn onto the road and the same lane we were in. In all fairness the speed limit was much lower and thus would've ordinarily provided enough time for the driver to determine a safe merge into our lane. We were simply going too fast around the wide curve for any driver to see us coming- even in the dark of night, even with our headlights on. Before I could react, before Graham could fully react, we made contact the sedan. In a fraction of a second, I could see the heads of the driver and the passengers of the car as the two collided. Most likely, the sound of the collision resonated throughout both vehicles because it was temporarily deafening to me. Both cars crumbled quickly under the impact although I'm sure the makers of each would be proud they both were able to withstand such an impact. The angle in which we struck the sedan as it was rolling onto the road caused the impact to occur right at the front end of the driver's side of their car and the front passenger side of ours. The airbags deployed, smacking the both of us in the face and furthermore, blocking most of our view. Graham, after yelling out an expletive, did his best to steer out of the way afterwards with the mangled tire from the passenger side. His over-correction sent us barreling left across the lane going in the opposite direction, past their shoulder and off into the wooded area, down a steep hill. Unfortunately the airbags had done their job for the day, offering no additional protection from the trees. We hit one specifically which caused us to bounce and hit another tree on the driver's side. Glass smashed and we continued down the hill at a slower rate yet, still out of control. It's fast when you're out of control. Graham extended his arm that now had small cuts on it in an attempt to protect me from bouncing around too much. I thought I heard my own neck pop three good times. I grabbed him as well, leaning over the console and we both ended up huddling together, suffering the violent bumps and hearing each subsequent impact, twist and the coupe endured as it sailed down the steep terrain.

CHAPTER FIFTEEN

My eyes were shut as tight as possible. I assume the car finally came to a stop because with the exception of a slight whizzing noise coming from the engine– there was silence. I opened my eyes to see Graham slumped over and more than enough blood on his now deflated airbag to make me uncomfortable. I called his name several times as I leaned over the console and moved him by the shoulders to get him seated straight and facing forward. I struggled somewhat to get out of my seatbelt, cutting myself a few times with the shards of broken glass that were every– where. Graham was unconscious with some minor cuts on his face that I could easily see, even in the darkness. I quickly checked his carotid pulse, applying my index and middle fingers to the upper portion of his neck. I had to temporarily suspend my own heavy breathing and calm my nerves so I could feel any pulse. This included my own mumblings to him, begging that he'd wake up. I heard only faint breaths from him.

I felt a slight thud against my fingers which by now had a little of his blood on them. I took another deep breath before I began counting each of those thuds, which would give me some indication into his well–being or lack thereof. It was barely pal– pable but translated into about forty beats per minute– a number I'd feel much better about if he were actually conscious and had not just violently rolled down hill. Without any hesitation, I started talking to him while at the same time feeling his head and face in the darkness for any signs of trauma.

"*Graham, I'm here . . . we've stopped. Please, please wake up, it's okay . . . I'm here,*" I said as I moved my hands over his face, to his chest, shoulders and arms as I gave them a squeeze. My own pains erupted and tears started to flow. This was too much for me, my mind raced and I started gasping for air. I couldn't do much for him at all sitting in this ravine which from the looks of the darkness hosted nothing but tall, mature trees. Graham's chest rose slightly– signaling his continued breathing however his eyes remained close. I automatically leaned over and kissed his forehead with en–

thusiasm while giving his arm a good squeeze. Nothing felt dislocated or broken so I assumed his unconsciousness was a result of the trauma from the Cadillac's contact with the trees. I was leaning over to Graham to cradle him in my arms– to soothe him. I checked for any possible swelling and moved my fingers again to monitor his pulse until I could figure out how we'd get to safety when I heard a couple voices yelling from the road above. The voices sounded like that of a man and a woman. I'd be surprised if they were the same folks from the car we just tagged because it wasn't an easy ordeal they'd just been through either.

"Hello! Are you okay down there?" I heard a male voice say. I immediately yelled in response, giving a somewhat faint but high pitched yell for help. They may or may not have heard my voice beyond the interior of the car because of the distance we were from them. Trying not to get frantic, I knew at any second the pickup truck would pull up and attempt to overdo any recapture efforts so I focused my efforts into reviving Graham.

Within a few seconds, through the back window my eye caught the flickering lights coming from the top of the hill where we lost control. The lights bounced around and got larger as they followed our same pathway down the ravine, quickly approaching our wrecked vehicle. I said a quick prayer hoping that the lights belonged to anyone left alive in the world except Davenport and his men. It could very well be them and everything would be up. I didn't have the strength to fight them all on my own. It would mean that everything we just went through was pointless and the only thing that came out of the deal was a serious injury to Graham. I leaned into him, and felt the metal of the gun in my jacket press into my stomach. If it was Davenport, my only objective for now was protecting Graham in his vulnerable state. As the flashlights came closer I could barely see the figures holding them so I opted to reach for the zip pocket with one hand. I yanked down on the little zipper and dug my hand into my side to grip the handle. I knew the safety was on, so with my thumb, I fumbled to release it. The nearest of the two lights dropped down behind the car as a hand hit the trunk to slow down whoever it was now that they'd made it. I jumped a little as a second later– another hand hit the trunk. I contemplated whether or not I should start shooting right away or wait until they walked up close enough for me to aim. Davenport and his men had more than enough firepower and ammo– they'd light the remainder of this coupe up with bullets until they were sure we were done for so I decided to wait and catch at least one of them off guard. For all I knew, they had no clue I was also armed. I kept my hand in my pocket– vowing to pull it out only without the gun in hand to help move Graham and with the gun to give it my best shot at taking the bastards out. Graham's chest rose slightly again. I gave him a slight squeeze and mumbled, "It's okay baby, just hold on."

Within a short second a head peered down into the broken window on the driver's side followed by a flashlight which was first shined on Graham's unconscious face and then on to mine. A second man showed up at my passenger side window. Neither of them appeared to be a part of Davenport's little army because the first thing they said did not consist of, 'Put your hands up'. Instead the man on the driver's side said, "Holy shit– is he still alive?"

"He's unconscious, but he's breathing." I responded, not removing my hand from my pocket just yet. I looked at the man's face, from the light I could see he was slightly heavyset, wore a dark long–sleeved shirt and cap. He had enough beard growth to look like he hadn't shaved in about two– weeks.

The man on the passenger side said nothing and started to check whether the door on my side would open when the other guy told him to hold on. "It's important that you answer us honestly– cause if not, be it now or later– we will shoot you. Have either of you been bitten, or scratched by those things?" The man next to Graham said flashing his light back and forth between the two of us. I knew my eyes weren't completely cleared up from all the broken blood vessels but I did my best to divert my attention.

I hesitated, looking at Graham as he let out a breath of air, his chest went down slightly but it was enough to catch all of our attentions in the silence he provided for my response. "No . . . We're good here." I said. I was, until I fall behind on a dose.

"Would you be willing to let one of my female comrades check you over just to be sure?"

"Of course." I replied as applied the safety and moved my hand out of my zip pocket and closed the zipper again. My training kicked back in as I used my both of my hands to straighten Graham's head so he had every opportunity for an unobstructed airway. I paid little attention to all of the glass around us as I heard the sound of the pieces falling on top of each other and onto the leather seat every time I moved. I turned to the door on my side and tried to open it. I had no luck even with the guy on the other side pulling it too. He ended up using a small branch to clear the rest of the broken glass and helped me climb out through the window. Once I was out, we both went over to the driver's side.

"By the way, my name is Wes, he's Dustin." The man with the dark long sleeves informed me once I was out of the car. I was a little unsteady at first, stumbling to gain my balance. The light from the two flashlights revealed dents and scrapes on nearly every square inch on the once–magnificent coupe. Pieces of tree branch were lodged in almost every surface that would catch them.

"I'm Seanna– this is my boyfriend, Graham." I said while tending to Graham's lightly bloodied face.

I noticed we were quite a ways down the ravine, at least three hundred feet in my guess. There was a definite path our car took that left a crooked little line easily seen in the darkness. I looked back into the car while Wes and Dustin attempted to open up the door. With some pulling from both of them, the door opened only partially due to a large dent that prevented the door mechanism's full rotation.

Graham was still secured in his seat belt as I reached for him to carefully pull him forward. To all of our surprise he let out a sigh that carried a little moan. I immediately went in and held his head gently, calling out his name, informing him of what we were doing. I told Wes to be careful as I unlatched his seat belt and Wes worked to carefully move his legs. The three of us were all intermingled as Dustin attempted to lift Graham's body while I guided his head in a synchronized fashion out of the car.

It was likely that three or four bullets whizzed past us hitting both the tree and the car before it registered to us, we were being shot at. The sound from the long range only provided a whizzing noise. It was the impact to follow that instructed us to quickly get moving.

"What the hell?" Wes yelled as he dropped Graham's legs and hurried for cover. Dustin was right behind Wes– moving toward a nearby tree as a bullet impacted the door right behind where we were all leaned in. I could barely move in time but I took care to not leave Graham in the shooter's line of sight. Instead of diving to get out of the way, which made way more sense; I squinted to see three or four figures moving around alongside the road where our car previously made its way down the ravine. I saw a long automatic rifle being aimed by two of the men along the bush as they readied themselves for continuous fire. I swore under my breath as I cautiously placed Graham's head back on the head rest and went for the tree a few feet nearby. Wes shoved his flashlight in the side pocket of his pants because it was still on and was visible through the fabric. I had a sinking feeling on top of all the nervousness and anxiety from all of the things I had endured.

"Must be scavengers!" Dustin assumed as he peeked around the edge.

"How the hell would they know we're down here? They would only see our car from the road up there." Wes reasoned.

"I hope Dana got out of there before they saw her." Dustin said.

I didn't look either of them in the face when I saw them instinctively pull out their guns. They were both holstered and to be honest I didn't even notice they had them from the position I was in, until now. I knew I saw a woman in the car when we hit them and assumed that's who Dana had to be. Wes whispered to Dustin– I barely heard him but it was something about readying themselves to fire if they shot at us again, just a few shots so they'd know we were armed and hopefully they'd move on instead of risking injury. I felt for my own weapon as I looked at Graham who was still in the same position we left him in. I knew who we were up against and that it would be wise to not shoot. It would save their lives to tell Wes and Dustin to leave instead.

I whispered to them to just take off as Wes whispered to shoot on his mark once he saw them advance down the hill. The men covered each other from what I could see. Out of the four, only two moved at a time. They advanced a few more paces before Wes gave Dustin the signal to fire a few rounds. Though it appeared no one was hit, all movement stopped briefly after that. Wes yelled out into the woods in their direction in a firm but calm manner.

"There's nothing down here but a wrecked vehicle! There's nothing of value here– if you continue to shoot– so will we! Your best bet is to go on somewhere else!"

It was a good effort on his behalf. If they were truly scavengers looking for something of value any other group might've thrown in the towel and ascended back up the hill. Unfortunately, only I knew for sure that was not the case. I knew they were going to continue down the hill and eliminate Wes and Dustin. My better judgment took over and forced me to go into action. I wanted no one else to get injured.

"I think we should just back up and let them see there's nothing down here. It's just Graham there injured. They'll see that and hopefully leave!" I whispered loudly.

I didn't give them the opportunity to protest. I knew in about two hundred feet they'd be on us and that would be the end of story. I got up from my crouched position and pulled them in the opposite direction from where the men were descending. I pulled them by their sleeves as they attempted to make the least amount of noise to let our intruders know we'd actually left. Within a second or so, Wes was actually in front of me as I whispered for him to turn his flashlight off. He was successful in doing so because in about two seconds I could barely see either of them, only trees and low hanging branches when I was immediately upon them and had to duck. I turned when I saw the silhouette of Wes turn and eventually we were headed slightly east and north from the site of the car wreck from a few minutes of jogging. I almost ran past them both when Dustin grabbed my arm and swung me around to where they hid. 'Ssshh . . .' was all I heard once I regained my footing, crouched down and waited. In the darkness I could see them both observing in movement from where we just came. It was the sounds of the crickets and other night time insects in the distance that filled my ears with noise. I had to swat at some insect crawling on my face.

It was the second time that happened this evening.

I looked down at my watch, bringing my wrist inches from my face but in the darkness I couldn't tell what time it was. It seemed at any moment it would be time for an injection, I felt it was time thirty minutes ago before we ended up in the spot we were in. Wes and Dustin remained focused on the direction from which we came while I remained focused and sensitive to any change in the way I was feeling. Of course it would be the most inconvenient time and place to break down but I'd rather know it was coming versus something unexpected. We waited there for at least five minutes. The occasional bite and irritation of various bugs perhaps was what got Wes, ready to go back.

"If they followed us, we'd have heard them by now," Wes said as he scratched his arm and stood up.

"Hopefully, I'd almost rather get shot at than slowly eaten up by these mosquitoes." Dustin replied.

"You guys stay low and quiet behind me. We'll zigzag our way back toward the area." Wes instructed. Within seconds we took off again at a slower pace to return to the site where the car was. Wes went ahead of Dustin, whom I was close behind. Wes paid extra attention to the area around us as he slowed his pace even more while cautiously approaching the space behind the tree where we initially hid. We were probably only a few yards away because the steep incline was very visible even in the darkness. Wes came to a stop and looked over near the road and pointed. Dustin and I caught up to him and looked over toward the road because of voices and what sounded like the arrival of another vehicle when we heard the noise from multiple doors being slammed closed.

"You guys stay put. I'll go check on your boyfriend, see if he's still breathing and all." Wes said.

"No, I'm a medic– I'll do it." I protested as I stepped in front of him.

"No, I'm a better shooter. Anyone can check a pulse," Wes argued.

I felt offended and started to object but two things stopped me at the same time. Three men appeared at the top of the hill whose long barreled rifles I could see from where we were. The second thing was the wretched pain which made my nervous system go into overdrive. I gritted my teeth as more perspiration built up instantly along my forehead. Wes probably took it as a concession as I simply muttered, "Fine, go ahead."

Wes stayed low as the men at the top of the hill grew in number to six. Neither of them moved or attempted to descend down the ragged path, they only peered down the hill and spread out as if to keep watch. I could hear voices but nothing comprehendible. Wes returned to us quicker than expected and leaned into us to report. My ears heard what he said but my mind could not grasp the meaning.

"*What?*" I automatically questioned.

"He's not there. They took him."

I looked around us in all directions, hoping Graham would pop out of nowhere because he woke up and saw them coming right after we left. I saw nothing but the dense outline of leaves and branches in the darkness, not a figure of a human being in sight– unless I looked in a certain direction up the ravine again. My eyes began to fill with tears and my breathing labored as my thoughts raced. I couldn't imagine what they'd do my Graham once they got him back to NGT. I covered my face with my hands for about two seconds until anger built up– which made my face fill up with heat. I thought about my pistol conveniently nearby. I reached in my zip pocket again, pulled out the pistol and stood up. Wes reacted quickly and with a sweeping motion placed both of his hands on my shoulders to basically sit me down. He was about the same height as Graham– which was taller than me.

"Listen! I don't know you and I don't know what you got going on with those assholes up there but that will do nothing but make things worse!" Wes said in an audible whisper. My vision was blurry from the tears still but I saw perfectly his point. A confrontation would serve no better purpose than add to the list of those already injured or dead. I took another deep breath as Dustin put his hand on my shoulder.

"You know those guys, don't you?" Dustin asked.

I only nodded my head, which I was sure they both could see in the darkness. They both let out sighs of frustration. Without faulting them, I expected both of them to stand up and haul themselves away from me and the whole situation. They didn't move. Instead they turned their attention to the voices from the top of the ravine again. This time it was clear they were going to descend down the hill. It was their movements that sparked a response from me.

"We're not fugitives or anything. We just wanted to leave." I whispered in urgency.

More voices and movements came from the hilltop again.

"You two were held against your will or something?" Wes questioned.

"Yes."

Wes contemplated only a second longer before declaring in a collected manner, "We should get moving." he straightened his hat further on his head and checked the gun already in his hand.

"Wait, I need to check the car for something. It's important– I'll go this time." I said. By now, with the pain slightly subsided I left no room for disagreement. I got up on both feet as I said it and darted around them both. Unfortunately the men started down the hill with flashlights in hand, searching the area around each tree before progressing down further. I made it to the car which the door was already opened from the driver's side where Graham once sat. Had it not been for the impossibly steep and crooked path the car took down the ravine they would've noticed my movements. I used it to my advantage and worked carefully to move the seat forward and retrieve the bag from the back seat. There was glass everywhere still as I leaned into the body of the car and frantically felt around for the bag. It wasn't a large bag yet it was big enough for me to know it was no longer there. I quickly felt the floor mats on the bottom thinking perhaps the bag got jammed under the seat during our descent but there was nothing that size. Instead, I felt quite a few tubular items lying on the floor. I grabbed one quickly and lifted up close enough to my face to know that it matched the one that was hopefully still intact in my jacket. With a renewed sense of urgency I leaned forward again to quickly gather every tubular item I could get my hands on. Within two seconds, I had to pull my hand back in order to put them all in my pocket. I was already reaching for more when I heard a loud whisper from Wes.

"Come *on!*"

I said nothing, yet only worked faster to scoop up more of the syringes that were nearly all under the passenger seat. I grabbed one more handful and yet another as I cut my fingers repeatedly on the broken glass strewn all over the floor. It was only when I saw the flicker of the approaching flashlights that I stopped my search, backed out of the car and back stepped as quickly as I could to get to the tree.

My bloodied hands were still gripping some of the syringes as I met up with Wes and we all took off as quietly as we could without rustling any branches. If it weren't for the humidity, the smaller branches would've cracked noisily under our feet. Dustin followed behind me as I tried to keep up with Wes, staying in the same path that he did in short, quick steps. The trees were unforgiving as they hindered our progress for a straight trail. We veered north from the site of the car and eventually jogged for what felt like a several blocks. A few times I stumbled and lost my pace but Dustin with his smaller stature, was right there to help me up and keep me moving.

We were all nearly out of breath and energy by the time we stopped– which was only for a few seconds. We turned left and went underneath a small concrete bridge that was likely a part of the same road we traveled on a short time before the crash.

It seems we'd been running alongside the highway for the most part.

"She knows what to do. She'll meet us at our designated place. Knowing her, she'll probably beat us there." Wes said in response to my inquiry about Dana.

"She ain't no Olympian but she's fast!" Dustin added under a heavy breath.

We headed under the bridge and jogged through more forest. It seemed as if we would run until our hearts stopped– in which case mine would certainly be the first. It was a few moments later at a spot in between a small clearing that I was forced to stop. My legs pretty much gave out and down I went. Poor Dustin had to hop over me or else he would've tripped over me. The pain returned and I could do nothing about it. I yelled out an expletive and nearly balled into a fetal position right there in the woods. Wes cursed as well, and rushed to stand over me. He turned on the flashlight and partially covered it so as not to attract too much attention should any harmful presence be nearby.

"What happened?" I heard him ask.

"Nothing, she just fell." Dustin replied.

I held out my hand which still had a grip on five or six syringes. My arm shook as I used the light he provided to select one of the syringes that were uneven in number; two pain medicines and four of the unique antiviral. Wes held on to the rest of them as I took the antiviral and lazily jabbed the needle in my arm after exposing my shoulder. Within a minute I could feel the racing force in my nerves slow as the flow of perspiration stopped and my breathing slowed again. I put my fingers on my own pulse and soon felt it go back to below normal again. The pain slightly subsided which was going to have to suffice for the time being. After another minute or so I was ready, Dustin helped me up, pulling me by my wrists at my requests because my hands were likely still bleeding from earlier.

Wes was irritated but dusted off my jacket before he handed back the syringes and told me it wouldn't be much farther to go. He paused for a second– as did I, before I figured out he probably wanted an explanation for the episode I just had.

"I have a condition. I'll explain later." I mumbled. Without giving any eye contact, I steadied myself to look in the direction we were headed beyond a small pathway through numerous mature Shortleaf pine trees. Wes shrugged at Dustin and continued on, not sprinting this time but walking quickly. Dustin stayed behind me again. We took off this time in a westward direction for only a few more minutes before it was clear we arrived at our destination.

Before us in the pitch of night stood a medium sized wooden shed that sat awkwardly by its self. There weren't any other buildings around– at least from first glance that it could possibly store anything for. Wes and Dustin quickly inspected the building around all sides before they came back to an unlocked side door and cautiously went in. I looked around as well trying to get a sense of direction and to catch my breath when the all clear was given and I stepped inside. The interior of the shed wasn't much larger than a standard room. The inside was dark, dusty and smelled identical to an old basement. There was no electricity but the outline of a table with a folded newspaper and standard tools lay on it. Dustin told me to hang out in here until I felt better while he went with Wes who apparently was already behind the shed. I pretty much ignored his offer to rest and instead followed behind him to see what Wes was doing.

Due to the direction we came from it was impossible to see what was behind the small building. Behind it however, was a small red Plymouth station wagon which Wes was already working on with only the minimal light from the flashlight. Like the shed, the car was old and equally dusty. Wes had opened the hood and with the flashlight in hand– was tugging at various wires. Dustin went behind the wheel, perhaps to try to start it on cue. I was likely unable to help much but took a look under the hood to see an extreme decline of the whole mechanical portion from its former glory days– which was probably around the same year I was born.

"Okay, give it a try." Wes said right before Dustin turned the ignition and the engine struggled before giving out.

"It won't turn over." Dustin said out of the window.

"That's because the thing needs spark plugs, at the very least." Wes muttered.

"And a miracle." a female voice spoke from behind us. I probably would've fallen forward from being startled but the car was in the way. I turned around as out from the trees nearby appeared a noticeably physically fit woman of about fifty whose pre-sence was nearly imaginary– even while she carried a brown paper bag in her hand. In a half–second, I knew it was Dana, the female passenger I saw briefly as our cars collided. Now that she was right next to me– I could understand why Dustin had con-fidence in her ability to return to this predetermined location alone and alive. Some people exude a presence that says they're a force to be reckoned with. Dana was no exception. She was still breathing heavy from her run as she stepped in and took a skeptical look under the hood.

"Yeah, it's still busted . . . Piece of crap. What's up with all the gunfire earlier?" Dana asked as she caught her breath. I could see the sweat beads across her fore-head as she sat her paper bag down and readjusted the ponytail of her long brown hair. From the light of the flashlight Dana had a few freckles that were partially blended in with well tanned skin on her arms. Her jean shirt sleeves were cut off at the should-ers which were probably more muscular than other women her age. The accent in her voice sounded Virginian and she ignored me completely as she walked around Wes to look at the engine from the other side.

"Well, we're nothing but bait out here until we can get it running. The gunfire was definitely unprovoked. We'll have to figure that out later." Wes replied as he used his fingers to wipe the dust off of a random wire.

They both went into some discussion unfamiliar to me that ultimately involved cleaning the spark plugs, something about finding a wrench and hopes about wires not being chewed by rodents. Dana was a few inches taller than Wes so he offered no protest when she told him to hurry and get on the ground to look from underneath to check the under carriage for rodent damage.

"Who are you?" Dana said to me casually after a few seconds.

"I'm Seanna. Sorry about earlier." I said referring to the accident.

"We can't worry about it now. We'll let the insurance companies figure out who was at fault. You all took quite a tumble down that hill." she said. She introduced herself and asked about the other person in the car with me.

"I don't know, they took him." I told her as I suddenly lost the distraction keeping my mind off of what happened earlier. I could see Dana's eyes narrow at the news. I could tell she was going to scrutinize my situation as she automatically looked around in the direction from where she came.

"They didn't look like law enforcement but they were armed like they were– that's why I got the hell out of dodge when I saw them pull up with all those guns. You better not be putting us all in danger." Dana said as she quickly turned from friendly to un-friendly in two seconds flat. Perhaps she was just being protective. Somewhere along the line I knew this would get really ugly if I didn't justify my existence with this group.

The fact was, I had a good reason to leave this group for their safety.

"Like I told Wes, *yes* those guys were after us. We took nothing from them so we owe them nothing. They were holding us against our will and we wanted to leave. That was the condensed version, but nevertheless– the basic truth." I explained to Dana and to Wes and Dustin again. She looked me in the eyes with the same skepticism as she did with the this old ragged wagon and probably with the same confidence she thought it would get us on the road again. I returned her stare, thankful that it was still pitch black, making it extremely difficult to see any remaining blood lining my irises. There was an awkward few seconds before Dana spoke up. Without her taking her eyes off of me she told Wes to clean the spark plugs.

"You'll pay if you bring us any trouble, you hear me? They'll no longer be your biggest problem." Dana warned.

"I have no bad intentions, ma'am."

"Now go see if there's anything else in that shed we can take with us while we try and get this crap can running."

Feeling like a child that had just been disciplined, I walked away before I was called back by Dana. She dug inside the pocket of her shorts and handed me a small flash-light. Inside the shed the walls were covered with rusted metal tools. They were likely just as dull and would take much longer to restore. I heard the sound of tools being used outside and Wes mumbling inaudibly from where I was. It was probably about me. I would assume he was telling Dana about my brief collapse on the way here and the events including the exchange of gunfire that happened before. I picked up various usable items such as a hammer, some rope– which again reminded me of Graham, and a box of nails that caught my eye on a shelf.

Dana's warning played over and over again while I pawed through the junk in the shed. Dana scared me. It was either her height or her voice or maybe both which en-hanced the persona but it was common sense that told me not to rile her. I had no clue where we would even go if and when the car was in working condition. Not knowing was only adding to the mountain of other issues that needed to be solved. I decided I would only stay with them for as much of the time as I needed to figure out how I would negotiate Graham's release and treatment of his wounds. More importantly, the amount of medication I had would tell me exactly how much time I had.

Feeling around in my pockets, I took out every syringe I had to get an official count. Two of the needles from the syringes taken from my jacket were likely broken from my fall and the contents leaked from their plastic wrapper and were nearly empty as I laid out everything on the dusty table. I sorted the syringes into two sections, one side for pain management and the other was the antiviral. I counted and then recounted both sides. I knew roughly I'd stuffed about ten syringes in each pocket before I had to leave and it was true. The tiny three milliliter syringes were about thirty in number– thanks to large jacket pockets that also carried tiny square bits of glass from the busted car windows as well. Fortunately the small handgun took up very little space for how heavy it was.

The final count was twenty-two and seven with the majority being the antiviral. I smiled a little because I would much rather be in pain than spiral out of control and possibly have the virus take over like what happened before. I was in the middle of carefully placing them back in the available space of my pockets when Dustin came into the shed. He was unfazed by what I was doing and instead focused his attentions on the hammer and rope. He then looked over at what was left on the table.

"Must be something pretty serious, huh?" Dustin said.

I nodded my head in agreement as I placed the last of them all back into my pockets. Dustin looked around to see if there were any more things they could use. He found a plastic bag balled up and offered it to me to put the medications in.

"Thanks, but that's how I lost the rest of them. I'll really have to hold on to this or else I'll be in trouble."

"Don't worry about Dana, we call her Momma Bear cause she's so protective."

"She should be– I don't blame her." I told him. It appeared to me that Dustin was probably no older than eighteen. His blonde hair, narrow eyes and adolescent face suggested all he needed was a skateboard and an iPod and he would be back in his element again. Instead, he too was forced to deal with the unfavorable fate that humanity was headed towards.

"Sweet, a universal socket wrench!" Dustin said as he reached across the table and grabbed the rusted tool that I would've ignored otherwise. He put the tool in his pocket just as the sound of a scuffle came from outside. Someone or something hit the side of the shed with a loud thud and shook the whole structure. Dustin and I ran outside and around the back side to see Dana and Wes in a struggle with a dead woman. The woman's face was nearly unrecognizable as only one eye was intact. She wore dirty, ripped up sweatpants and a flannel shirt. Her brown hair was matted with blood and dirt and she was entirely focused on Wes. The gurgling groans that came from her were disgusting and even more wretched was her ceaseless attempts to attack Wes would've easily overpowered her except she was on his back and he was using his hands to keep her head away from his skin. Dustin motioned me to stay put as he pulled Dana off from helping, pulled out his gun and aimed for the woman's head. In the dark he focused on his target, with both hands on his weapon and gave the trigger a squeeze. The struggling stopped as Wes fell to his knees and the dead woman released her grip. Instantly, she slid off of Wes and hit the ground like literal dead-weight. I ran over to Wes and smelled the same rotted meat and clay odor from my own previous encounters.

Wes said nothing but as soon as I touched him, he jumped. I tried to soothe him but he yelled, "Back the hell off!"

Dana stepped in now, insisting to see if he'd been injured. Wes was a little less resistant toward her as she motioned for me to come and look him over. Dustin stood watch as we both looked through his ripped shirt in multiple places but fortunately saw no broken skin. The blood on his neck appeared to be from the woman as we hurried to clear it from infecting him.

"Where did she come from?" Dustin asked.

"It doesn't matter. We need to leave now. That gun fire will either draw more of 'em or bring Seanna's buddies to our location. The car wreck is less than a mile from here." Dana replied.

Dustin ran for the driver's seat of the car but by then Wes was on his feet and told him he'd try and start it. Wes was obviously shaken by the attack but focused on his newest task with renewed diligence. He cursed and grumbled under his breath for the car to start and on the forth try, the engine stuttered to life. Truthfully, the thing sounded like it would cut off at any second but Wes kept his foot on the gas every time any weakness in its running occurred.

Dana hollered for us to get moving as we all rushed into the small wagon. Dana grabbed her bag and I ran back into the shed for the hammer, rope and syringes before I hurried to the back seat next to Dustin. Wes put the old wagon into drive and turned the headlights on. There was an awkward path barely visible due to the over-growth of trees and bushes which likely had been untended since long before the out-break. The path eventually opened up a half-mile or so later where it became a paved road in the middle of a large clearing where we saw seemingly unoccupied houses on both sides. I didn't bother with a seat belt, which I should've known better after all I've just went through. Instead, I pressed down on the silver metal lock mechanism for the door on my side. Dustin saw me and did the same thing for his door.

Hoping to see her face, instead I looked at the back of Dana's head and leaned forward to both her and Wes.

"Where are we going?" I asked above the roar of the engine as we finally hit smooth pavement, passed an intersection and in my estimation headed west down another dark, two-lane road.

Dana kept her gaze straight ahead and replied, "We're going to safety."

ABOUT THE AUTHOR

Whenever she's not preparing for the apocalypse, Ms. Daniels is reading, blogging, clipping coupons or tending to a childlike, Labrador-mix dog she calls, Oliver.

Dottie currently resides in Minneapolis, Minnesota.

VISIT THE AUTHOR

Publisher:
dpInk: DonnaInk Publications: http://www.donnaink.com

Author Websites
http://www.authordottiedaniels.com

Facebook
https://www.facebook.com/pages/Author-Dottie-Daniels

Twitter
http://www.twitter.com/authorddaniels

WordPress
http://authordottiedaniels.wordpress.com
https://dottiedaniels.wordpress.com

Affliction

by Dottie Daniels

dpInk: DonnaInk Publications
www.donnaink.com

SIGN UP FOR MERCHANDISE

If you would like to get on Dottie Daniels mailing list for future T-Shirt, poster, mugs, etc. email: affliction@donnaink.com. Dottie is featuring a suite of merchandise and perhaps — you can visit herWordPress blog and join the followers she has there as well.

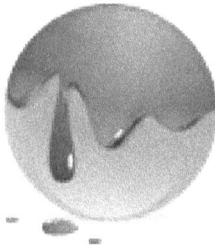

dpInk
Donnalnk Publications, L.L.C.

Publisher
www.donnaink.com

For bulk orders, special orders, etc.
Special Markets Division
dpInk: Donnalnk Publications, L.L.C.
129 Daisy Hill Road
Carthage, North Carolina 28327
Email: special_markets@donnaink.com

For Promotions:
Promotions Division
dpInk: Donnalnk Publications, L.L.C.
129 Daisy Hill Road
Carthage, North Carolina 28327
Email: promotions@donnaink.com

ZENCON ART OF
ZEN CONSULTANCY
PR & Marketing

www.ingramcontent.com/pod-product-compliance
Lightning Source LLC
Chambersburg PA
CBHW050506210326
41521CB00011B/2351